MYTH AND MODERNITY IN THE TWENTIETH CENTURY ROMANIAN NOVEL

Ileana Orlich

EAST EUROPEAN MONOGRAPHS, BOULDER, COLORADO
DISTRIBUTED BY COLUMBIA UNIVERSITY PRESS, NEW YORK
2009

EAST EUROPEAN MONOGRAPHS, NO. DCCXLV

ISBN: 978-0-88033-643-7

Library of Congress Control Number: 2008938731

Printed in the United States of America

ACKNOWLEDGMENTS

I would like to begin by expressing my sincere gratitude to the National Endowment for the Arts that awarded a portion of my project a literary translation grant. I am also grateful for the research opportunities offered by a Fulbright scholarship during my sabbatical year, and for the summer grants awarded the Romanian Cultural Institute and the Arizona State University Institute for Humanities Research.

My special thanks go to Directors Livia Drăgoi of the National Museum of Art, Cluj-Napoca, and Doina Pauăleanu of the Museum of Art, Constanța, Romania, for their generosity in allowing me to share the art resources of their museums.

I would also like to acknowledge the help of Carl Ralston for his excellent work on this book.

CONTENTS

INTRODUCTION

Recovering Western tradition and simultaneously challenging realism as a dominant narrative mode, *Myth and Modernity in the wentieth-century Romanian Novel* conveys the shifting and subtle identities and continuities of literary tradition by opening up unfamiliar aesthetic and cultural landscapes through critical examinations of a distinctive and unusual range of writers and texts. Collectively, the book proposes to chart a series of imaginative cross-currents across the century's representative fiction while attesting to the importance of and necessity for a critical version of the Romanian novel and commitment to uncovering its dynamic interactions with a culture that was surrealist *avant la lettre*, modernist in orientation, and steeped in the magic of folklore and archaic myth.

Overcoming the lasting, tenuous grip of Realism, Romanian novelists of the twentieth century interrupted narrative conventions to offer in their fiction a re-positioning of language, a potent iconography, and a nationalist mythopoetic universe *vis-à-vis* modernity. As common ground for artists and novelists in the twentieth century, Romania provided a peculiar space to all fiction; a space that, when exported, gave definition to a good part of the twentieth century itself. The Romanian-born Tristan Tzara, the founder of the Dada movement, spoke indirectly about that peculiar milieu through his made up name – which means "sad in the country" - and about the specific longing of the artist's psyche.[1] It was a longing that gave birth to some of the twentieth-century's most influential Avante-garde experimentalism (Avant-gardism) and, as Tom Stoppard's play *Travesties* suggests, changed the way modern Europe thinks, looks, and dreams.[2]

In the decades preceding and following WWI, the provincial inventions of a coterie of young Romanian Avant-gardists such as Tristan Tzara, Marcel Iancu, Stephan Roll (born Gheorghe Dinu) Ilarie Voronca (born Eduard Marcus), and Victor Brauner in Bucharest appeared in short-lived but significant journals where their artistic frondistes' absurd poems gleefully absorbed their touchingly insane drawings. The list of publications includes: *75HP* whose single, 1924 issue, under the directorship of Ilarie Voronca and Victor Brauner, advocated the concept of pictopoetry; *Integral*, which started its publication in Bucharest under Benjamin Fondane and Hans Mattis-Teutsch until 1928, *Unu*, led by Saşa Pană and including in its 1928-1932 issues contributions not only from prominent Romanian Avant-gardists, but also poems of contributors like Louis Aragon, André Breton, René Crevel, and Paul Èluard, and rich art work illustrations from Marc Chagall and Man Ray, among many others; and *Contimporanul*, which started its publication in 1922 under the supervision of Ion Vinea and was in subsequent years responsible for organizing four surrealist exhibitions that hosted both Romanian and foreign surrealists.

Torn between taking for granted that an artist is a seer, a *voyant* in Rimbaud's words, and entertaining at the same time a vast sense of futility, artists of the Romanian Avant-gardism sought to free language from its conventions. It achieved this goal by demolishing, in aggressive shockwaves of experimental disruption, the supremacy of language, and by deferring playfully to their own intellectual and mystical qualities rooted in the vast, imaginary playing field of Levant - an approximate area of the Balkans, circumscribed by the Black Sea and consisting largely of Romania and parts of Bulgaria, the former Yugoslavia, Greece and Turkey - a peculiarly European-oriental region whose Byzantine attitude (unconventional sexuality coupled with a decadent *joie de vivre* in the face of adversity) and aesthetic impulses echoed throughout twentieth-century Romanian fiction.

Simultaneously, the Romanian fiction of the twentieth century was open to and receptive of Western influences that created conditions for the emergence of a robust Romanian Modernism. Promoted primarily by the critic and novelist Eugen Lovinescu through his influential magazine and literary cenacle *Sburătorul* (*Winged Spirit*; 1919-1927), the systematic adaptation of Western models in order to align Romanian literature and culture with its European counterparts was formulated in his "synchronism" theory. While opposing the "extremist trends" of the Avant-garde, Lovinescu's theory encouraged the synchronization of Romanian culture with its urban counterparts in Western Europe without discounting a need for cultural specificity, namely a national originality that would manifest itself naturally in the resulting fictional works. In his seminal histories of modern Romanian civilization and literature, *Istoria literaturii române contemporane (History of Contemporary Romanian Literature*) and *Istoria literaturii române contemporane*, 1900-1937 (*History of Contemporary Romanian Literature*, 1900-1937, 1937),[3] Lovinescu opposed the previous century's sentimental lyricism and romanticized rural fiction and promoted instead exploration and innovation in literature, as well as an emphasis on the urban environment and the probing of consciousness.

Exposed to both the literary excesses of the Avant-garde and the intellectual exchanges with the urban cultures of the West, Romanian novelists of the twentieth century were also devoted to the genius of genuine folk art. All of them drew their inspiration from the magic of the Romanian folklore that came to Romanian peasants nearly uninterrupted from Greece, and Byzantium, almost unbroken from Orpheus who was born in Thrace, and that transformed its metaphors, motifs, and archetypes. Such alchemical operations produced unique blends of folkloric realism and Gothic fantasy, an integration of formative Romanian myths and mythic folk types within Western canons of Modernism; and a continuous exchange between Western fictional models and Romanian folklore's genres, oral creations and forms (from the songs of longing known as *doine*, to ballads, legends, tales, and rituals).

The fictional configurations of the works selected in this volume reflect the subtle transformations and interplay of all these cultural models, from the experimental trends of the Romanian Avant-garde, through the creative imitations and explorations of Modernist tradition to the reliance on an indigenous rural or folk tradition. As national narratives that both absorb the literary value of oral creations and rely simultaneously on Modernist self-conscious aesthetic creations and established models of grand narratives, these selected works also conform to a national literary tradition that George Călinescu, one of the most respected twentieth-century critics, sought to establish in his *Istoria literaturii române de la origini până in prezent* (*History of Romanian Literature from Its Origins to the Present*, 1940).[4] Finally, the dynamics of trans-individual elements of these works – namely their types of discourses, images, themes, cultural clichés and other conventions that are ancillary to individual fictional creations, recommend the novels discussed in this volume as miniature canonical units that meet the "critical" norms the influential Romanian critic Nicolae Manolescu has established in his *Critical History of Romanian Literature* (1990).

Like his close friend and collaborator, the painter Victor Brauner who illustrated two of Naum's volumes of poetry, Gellu Naum absorbed Avant-garde experimentalism and turned it into an idiom for a private journey of initiation into a self-state, and for freeing what lay in the unconscious. With an *oeuvre* traversing the organic and the inorganic, between animal, vegetal, human and mechanical realms, Naum's poems, and especially his novel *Zenobia* (1985), the metadiscourse is a kind of feedback loop of poetic feeling that incorporates Brauner's painting, indicating that Brauner's painting influenced Naum's works as much as these works influenced Brauner's painting.[5] But while Brauner used in his paintings an autonomy that language (because of its endlessly referential quality of words and the rules of grammar) never allowed, Naum had to overcome the habitual uses of language to make his art and to conduct in his own work a search for his magical self using not only surreal imagery and erotic energies connected to pre-literate mythological motifs but also broader aesthetic and literary possibilities from established European cultures. In its seamless prose that structurally resembles poetic expression and thought, *Zenobia* combines a narrative adaptation of the Romanian and international Avant-garde with a Modernist text that echoes T. S. Eliot's *The Waste Land*, the expressive French Surrealism of the 1920s and 1930s, and André Breton's mystifying surrealist novel *Nadja*.

Like Breton's *Nadja*, *Zenobia* incorporates startling, juxtaposed images that could easily be painted and an abundance of corporeal imagery not much different from the visual products of the Surrealist painters like Brauner, whose works intimate that surreal states are best attained through sexual encounters with the erotic double. But unlike Breton whose *Nadja* has been criticized for its seemingly negative and exploitative views of women, Naum portrays in *Zenobia* a feminine double whose engagement in a wonderfully complex relationship with its male counterpart anticipates twentieth-century feminist perspectives.

In addition to its feminocentric orientation that corresponds to Luce Iregaray's view of woman as a "*sensible transcendental*"[6] and thus bridges in one more way the novel's Avant-gardism with Modernity, *Zenobia* also resonates with the modernistic techniques of *The Waste Land*, another work that juxtaposes strange and apparently disparate, surreal images rooted in the unconscious. In the peculiar atmosphere of *Zenobia*, and associated with the mystical universality of the Romanian cosmos, Naum foregrounds the Tiresias-like, ancestral character of Dragoş, whose assessment of the world from a one-eye perspective also transcribes into the novel Brauner's 1931 "Self-portrait" with one eye missing from a bleeding socket. Brauner's prophetic portrait painted before the real loss of the artist's eye during a fight[7], as well as his subsequent works that focus on the eye, suggest the same capability of seeing the future as plainly as the past, which Naum attributes to Dragoş in the profound and occult sense that Romanian Avant-gardists felt could be reached through their art.

Other significant modernist techniques are effectively displayed in Camil Petrescu's *The Bed of Procrustes*, a novel emblematic of the century's sexual anxiety and anesthesia and of the uninhabitable, fractured landscape that evokes a Procustean bed. The novel's parallel storylines animate male homosocial desire, a crisis of masculinity, and an acute dissociation of sensibility, akin to the "hysteric" disposition of T.S. Eliot's poetry and corresponding to his broodings in the famous essay praising the Metaphysical poets. In Petrescu's novel, the two male protagonists – a poet, whose cultural and personal anxieties both embody and perform male hysteria, and his modernist double, whose own sexual anxiety forges an hysteric identification with the poet that transcends male homosocial bonding – reflect modern man's aesthetic and cultural detachment and disembodiment that *The Bed of Procrustes*, following Baudelaire, Pound, and Eliot, ultimately delineates.

Integrating early twentieth-century Romanian novel into the European circuit in spite of its specific, ethnic origins, Hortensia Papadat-Bengescu's novels *Disheveled Maidens* (1926), *A Concert of Music by Bach* (1927), and *The Hidden Way* (1932)[8] interrupt Avant-garde experimentalism and follow the dictates of Lovinescu's Western-inspired theory of synchronism. A protégée of Lovinescu and a fixture at the literary gatherings he hosted every afternoon in his own house, Papadat-Bengescu carried out the critic's theories and revisionist aspirations in her own analytical fiction that focused on individual destinies and transformations and on shifting social environments. Conceptualized as a grand narrative that maps out Romania's progressive emancipation and democratization, the three novels that make up Papadat-Bengescu's Hallipa trilogy emphasize the importance of self-conscious aesthetic creation while relying on the inherited Western traditions of the realist, urban, and psychological narrative. As if performed on a stage, which is largely the Romanian capital of Bucharest between the wars, the novels offer a panoramic view of the political, cultural and economic context of Romania's institutions and society. The dynamics of the plot emerge in each novel from the use of such overlapping semiotic fields as text, music, fashion, architecture and interior design, industrialization, and even makeup and women's clothing. In Papadat-Bengenscu's fiction behavioral conventions are seen as a form of highly symbolic representations of the country's patriarchal society and cultural values, ideals, and aspirations, and of the writer's ambivalence in her views of gender, society in the interwar period, the trilogy tackles disruptive and traumatic domestic and social experiences reflected in the dissolution of the Hallipas' marriage; the growing emancipation of women discernable in the feminist tendencies of Mini, Lina Rim, Cora Perşu, Coca-Aimée, or the sexual awakening of Elena Drăgănescu; and political engagement and arrivism associated with the rise of characters like Lică the Trubadour (from penniless dandy to Parliament deputy) or the social climbing of Princess Ada and Jorj Drăgănescu.

The possible tensions between the cosmopolitan-modernist discourse of Papadat-Bengescu's fiction and the richness of the Romanian native myths and folkloric tradition promoted in the robust interwar journal *Gândirea* (*The Thought*, 1921-1944)[9], are transcended in the works of Mihail Sadoveanu, a novelist who revalorized the epic potential of Romanian folk ballads as a synthesis of local storytelling traditions (historical narratives, popular narratives, folktales) and Western influences. Sadoveanu's distinction between the literary and documentary value of folklore – "Not every folk production has value, only because it is popular. For the student of philosophy and folklore it may have value in itself; I, as a writer, am interested only in its brilliance –" underscores the literary value of oral creations while at the same time praising their potential as models of literacy akin to Western counterparts.[10]

Mixing folk motifs and nationalist themes with Modernist techniques and Western models, Sadoveanu's celebrated novels *The Hatchet* (1930) and *Tales from Ancuța's Inn* (1928)[11], propose a particularly engaging compositional type of narrative that adapts orality and literacy to modernist discourse. As one of the opposing paradigms that shape critic Nicolae Manolescu's view of literary history[12], we perceive the written versus the oral narration, and in each instance the intertwined texts allow for the coexistence and interaction of storytelling vis-à-vis orality and literacy. In investing his novels with the great energy required to re-trace over and over again such a well-known story as the *Miorița* ballad in *The Hatchet*, for example, Sadoveanu displays the independence of vision and personalization of creation that David Bordwell, in a different context, identifies and defines as the modernist impulse resulting from the association of a good story with innovation.[13] Undercutting the orally inflected expectations of social restoration, of a return to and confirmation of the traditional order after the murderers of the slain shepherd are punished, the readers of *The Hatchet*, who are most likely familiar with the *Miorița* ballad, find themselves weighed down all along by the same type of anxieties that the start of a traditional narrative journey typically forments: where is Vitoria Lipan (Sadoveanu's protagonist) going? Where will she end up? Will she make it? In legitimizing such questions in a retold tale that retains a stubborn vitality, Sadoveanu's story confers on the oral perpetuity of the ballad the new self-consciousness of archetypal characters (peasants, shepherds, cattle-dealers) born out of eminently eloquent narrative expression.

Engaging the readers in the shift from the orally inflicted space of Romanian country inns and storytelling communicated as recycled recollections, Sadoveanu's *Tales from Ancuța's Inn* makes further use of orality to project the cultural specificity of the Romanian inn into the confines of literacy. Like Harry Bailey's Tabbard in Chaucer's *Canterbury Tales*, Ancuța's Inn acquires in Sadoveanu's text a legitimacy found only in the literately inflected. The tendency to add a great deal of local color into a literately inflected narrative that brings together surreal prose and modernist techniques, complete with a scrambling of temporal and spatial categories, a propensity for irony and attention to the stylistic rather than the ideological aspects of the prose, and a free approach to language, reaches canonical heights in Stefan Agopian's novel *Velvet Tache* (1980).[14] With its chatty wisdom and monologic performance of a protagonist who writes his memoirs posthumously, *Velvet Tache* is an unforgettable account of a narrator who experiences all kinds of ruptures between the first-person narrating self and the experiencing self, and between the mythic space of childhood, nourished by the imagery of oral folk tales and fantastic historical accounts, and the alienating world of a tormented chapter in nineteenth-century Southwestern Romanian history. As the three parts of the book illustrate, Tache's journey from childhood through maturity and death, the narrative reveals, by implication, the shifts and readjustments of Romanian society in its fight for independence against the Ottoman Empire and its transition from patriarchal village culture (transmitted primarily through folklore, myth, and superstition) to incipient, modern statehood.

The chosen locale of *Velvet Tache* reveals a region of Romania that Agopian singles out, a region that he implies was obscured, lost, or effaced in other narrative and historical accounts. To read of such events as those the novel foregrounds from the inside of the protagonist Tache's mind, so to speak, gives readers a better understanding of what occurred and what has been lost in historical accounts of these events. In employing fiction as a means of examining and questioning history, *Velvet Tache* also proposes a narrative alternative history that develops a dramatic tale in the face of mounting political oppression. Published at the height of the dictator's regime of terror in Communist Romania, Agopian's novel challenges more than any other novel of the 1980s the dominance of the state-imposed Realism. The Southwestern province of Oltenia, which was, incidentally, the hated country leader Nicolae Ceausescu's own native region, offers a complex interplay between the novel's labyrinthine narrative, with its convoluted stories of the Romanian past infused with the magic of myth and folklore, and the larger implications of Tache's narrative. Its compensatory vision of reality attempts, in the established mode of Magical Realism, to create tranquility by reflecting on the absurdity of life and by presenting characters as pawns of unknown and powerful forces.

Whether they offer an interplay between a national tradition and cosmopolitan orientation, emphasize the importance of their innovative aesthetic production, or require a reconsideration of the role of folklore in the formation of the literary canon, the novels discussed in this volume cannot claim in their individual or collective examination anything more than a single (but not totalized) representation of what the nineteenth-century historian Nicolae Bălcescu called "ideas and sentiments of the time."[15] In this sense, far from commanding the notion of a single and all-embracing narrative, these works represent important exemplars, but not the only ones to stand for the richness of the twentieth-century Romanian novel.

CHAPTER 1

Romanian Avant-Gardism and French Surrealism Beyond *The Waste Land*: Gellu Naum's *Zenobia*

> We have lingered in the chambers of the sea
> By sea-girls wreathed with seaweed red and brown
> Till human voices wake us and we drown.
>
> T.S. Eliot, "The Love Song of J. Alfred Prufrock"

Scholarly commitment to Gellu Naum's work has acknowledged his affiliation with Surrealism, fueled in no small part by the Surrealists' indebtedness to Tristan Tzara, the flamboyant, Romanian-born Dadaist, and to the Romanian Avant-garde experimentalism (Avant-gardism) that included such luminaries of the movement as Ilarie Voronca and especially the painter Victor Brauner. In the same Dada-Romanian Avant-gardism-Surrealist circuit, Romanian critics have also commented on the connections between *Zenobia*, Naum's most celebrated work, and André Breton's *Nadja*, another equally mysterious, surrealist masterpiece.[1]

Although Naum (1915-2001) stated in an interview taken several decades after Breton's death that he could no longer bear to read him, he also insisted on praising the charismatic founder of surrealist ideology as the man who "brought together all the great ideas of the twentieth century, changed people's minds, indeed changed the world: "Take a look around you," Naum urged his interviewer, "and [you will] believe me that he [Breton] managed to shatter the old and false ideas – and that's no small task [my translation]."[2]

Published in 1985 and projected in an indeterminate time, *Zenobia* crystallizes the chief tenets of Surrealism that Breton formulated: correspondences between different realms from the unconscious to consciousness; an insistence on the omnipotence of dream and the necessity for man to incorporate the dream process into his waking state, as well as a belief in Breton's concept of *hasard objectif* (objective change or coincidence) as the means of liberating the psyche from its enslavement to reason by stringing together endless non-rational associations.

A "*prozopoem*"[3] whose narrative discourse, in the manner of Breton's *Nadja*, borders on poetic representation, *Zenobia* brings up the same unanswerable question formulated in Michel Beajour's "*Qu'est-ce que Nadja*?" In other words, is *Nadja* fiction or poetry?[4] From this perspective, *Zenobia* is, like *Nadja*, a new novel that, as

Carlos Lynes puts it, "has analogies with modern poetry as well as with a much earlier narrative tradition."[5] Such critical observations bring further significance to the understanding of both *Nadja* and *Zenobia* as artistic experiments in the surrealist tradition and substantiate their reading as modern poetry, by which I mean an unusually poetic and metaphorical prose whose lyrical descriptions flicker in and out of consciousness, drifting from mental image to actual event to transcend the relational.

With their fragmented structure and seemingly disconnected thoughts transitioning the last trace of transcendence into a realm of random montage with the quotidian life, and with their focus on the feminine element suggested in their titles, both *Nadja* and *Zenobia* are also reminiscent of *The Waste Land*, T. S. Eliot's eccentric poem that is equivalent in content to an epic,[6] and an unmistakable surrealist work[7] centered on relations with and observations of women. Its radically different structure may be seen as Eliot's contribution to the Surrealists' effort to subvert conventional art, and its concern with the feminine is suggested on (1) the poem's title which points unmistakably to a waste land that, in the mythic terms Eliot appropriated from Sir J. G. Frazer's *The Golden Bough* and Jessie Weston's From Ritual to Romance relates to the land as the feminine counterpart of a king or lord; and (2) the poem's epigraph which asserts a female symbol, the Sibyl of Cumae. Beyond such similarities, the London of *The Waste Land*, which is articulated with the discernable city imagery that recurred in French poetry from Baudelaire's onward,[8] is also as much the modern inferno and breeding-ground of lust and viciousness as Breton's Paris and Naum's Bucharest. Holding their authors' fascination, these urban landscapes are not merely a stage subordinated to the action; like post-war London, both Paris and Bucharest help direct the narrative action that takes on a dream-like, surreal and nightmarish quality. Such apparent parallels between *Nadja* and *Zenobia*, on the one hand, and *The Waste Land* on the other, elicit further examination and elucidation.

My purpose in this chapter is to explore first the rich topic of *Zenobia* vis-à-vis *Nadja* as surrealist works consolidated through the routing of Romanian Avant-gardism, and to focus on the two writers' claim that erotic life creates temporary states of transcendence achieved through an annihilation of quotidian consciousness. Furthermore, I propose to trace the previously neglected similarities of both *Nadja* and especially *Zenobia* to *The Waste Land*, another work where descriptions of pre-war London, like the metropolitan imagery of Paris and Bucharest, bring in a montage pattern whose random flickering coalesces into a modern perspective of multiplying figures and scenarios, and where ghosts occasionally walk the thoroughfares of the city making it difficult to decide which encounters are "irreducible"[9] events and which are visions, either waking or sleeping.

The very discussion of surrealist writing cannot begin without considering first the context of surrealist aspirations formulated by the movement's primary theoretician, André Breton. His insurrectionist dialectics, the motto "More consciousness!" that he borrowed from Marx to acknowledge the refusal to accommodate routine, and his insistence on defining Surrealism as "*un état du fureur*," became the foundation of Gellu Naum's own degree of theoretical rigor. Taken and adapted to his own manner in *Zenobia* – a work whose heroine embodies, in Naum's words, "the refusal of a false consciousness" – that powerful fury made Naum one of the most articulate apologists of Surrealism and further stimulated his form of surreal radicalism keeping it alive until the end of the twentieth century.

According to Breton, the aim of Surrealism was "to prevent the domination of the symbol by the thing signified." To help modern man rediscover the meaning and vitality of words, objects had to be changed from their habitual forms and remade as symbols. To rescue man from this state of alienation and delirious cacophony that degraded and prostituted language, Breton also proposed to actualize the magic of metaphor when he proclaimed in "Letters to Seers" that "what is will be, by virtue of language alone." In December 1924, the first of the surrealist manifestoes codified such ideas that had been, in fact, in gestation for almost a decade. For although the still-warm corpse of Dada is not mentioned once in Breton's manifesto, the urge to surrealist action takes its notes from Tristan Tzara's bold proclamations:

> I destroy the pigeon-holes in the brain and those of social organization; to demoralize everywhere and fling my hands from heaven to hell, eyes from hell to heaven, reestablish the fecund whirl of a universal circus, in powers that are real and rooted in each individual's fantasy.[10]

A Romanian poet of Jewish origin who had formally petitioned the Romanian government in 1929 to change his real name, Samuel Rosenstock, into Tristan Tzara,[11] Tzara was the quintessential Dada artist, whose aesthetics demand radical changes and whose role was to guide the Dada revolution. Having arrived on the scene in Zurich in 1916 as a reaction to WWI of radical leftist and anarchist intellectuals of different nationalities led by Tristan Tzara, Dada quickly became the high point of Western European culture as it carried to an extreme the unrestrained collective will that sounded the note of social protest and demanded political changes. As a radical project, Dadaism created its own genre, the manifesto, which was meant to change radically the life/art relation and to transform the figure of the artist into a brutal activist attached to (not detached from) life.

Although Tzara soon became Breton's main rival, his objectives anticipate Breton's own will to mock the bourgeois cocooned in his morality. Aiming for the creation of a purely novel society that buries the stiff corpse of European bourgeoisie and tramples on its sanctimonious morality, Tzara and the Dadaists presented themselves as daring elements ready to cure humanity of bourgeois dementia. Like Breton, Tzara displayed a high consciousness of the necessity of class struggle alongside his sublime affectations claiming that bourgeois society had completely lost the ability for invention in art and that bourgeois did not excite the imagination or sharpen thought.[12]

Even though the short-lived Dadaist fervor and Dadaism in general had faded from center stage as a mere aesthetic accident, a powerful political art flourished in their aftermath. With Dadaism vanished from the stage, Breton carried its blatant musculature of expression aiming to free human sensibility from its importunate training in bourgeois common sense and in the insipid quality of bourgeois culture. Echoing Tzara, Breton pleaded for an art that deliberately scrapped the border between artistic and political action, an art whose professed goal was to crash the monsters of imperialism, Victorian morals and prejudices, and classical art, and, while dismantling the system, prepared for the new reality that would bring the radical cohesion and merging of aesthetics and politics, ideology and reality, patriarchal and political structures.

Breton's "First Manifesto of Surrealism" can be viewed as an essential neo-Dadaist document that emphasizes the powers of imagination, a by-product of what Breton's friend Hugo Ball, in his diary for 1917, calls "the new art," (meaning Dada). Recognizable as Breton's implementation of the Dadaist project, Ball's call for "the will-to-the-image" expresses an estrangement from an existing order and the need to find a new direction, a direction that "...inclined to force the image, even though the means and parts be antagonistic...[a direction that] drives toward the in-dwelling, all-connecting life nerve, [and] is indifferent to external resistance."[13]

Although it reiterates some of the Dadaists tenets, the merit of Breton's Manifestoes lies in codifying such ideas and in giving them a proper sense and purpose of unified exploration, as opposed to the Dadaists' dead-ended forms of protest and self-mocking slogans.[14] In particular, the central idea expressed in the Manifestoes, apart from the omnipotence of dream and the necessity for man to incorporate the dream process into his waking state is Breton's recommendation, of great significance for a further understanding of *Nadja* and especially *Zenobia*, that in the interest of uncovering the surreal, indeed, that the real be approached and handled in certain ways. Thus, although it places immediate trust in certain surreal actions, Breton's 1924 text is in agreement with Eliot's own claim that "the material of art is always actual life"[15] and by no means limits access to the real. Here again, however, the methods and directions Breton proposes for prospecting the real bring forth the Dadaists' favorite technique – that of collage. Breton's variations of this technique account for the collage principles of disparate views of photos, interpretations or reports that induces in his work the impression of autonomy or casual interdependence and produces an art defying the sacral continuity and normative causality of events.

Also of interest for the study I propose in this chapter is Breton's pamphlet "The Surrealist Situation of the Object" (1953) in which he introduces the concept of *hasard objéctif* ("objective chance or coincidence"). Defined as "that sort of chance that shows man, in a way that is still very mysterious, a necessity that escapes him, even though he experiences it as a vital necessity," this concept is essential in the surrealist enterprise as the means of liberating the psyche from its enslavement to reason by stringing together endless non-rational associations. Ultimately, Breton's insistence on "objective chance" and the hallucinatory and irrational thought associations and recollected dream images of *Nadja* confirm that the full flowering of Surrealism (and of Breton the artist), is to be sought in the responses it solicits when such theoretical statements are incorporated in what is considered Breton's best fictional writing.

Before beginning to decipher Breton's celebrated *Nadja*, I want to take a closer look at Naum's surrealist ideology in order to bring into relief its mobile, fluid relationship to the Romanian Avant-gardism's and to Breton's model. Most importantly, I propose to show that Naum's preoccupation with the unconscious mind, the operations of chance, and the collage technique, as well as his systematic experimentation with the language, point to both the convergence and the differences amongst their ideas and narrative techniques.

In the years before WWII, Naum was closely connected to the figures of the Romanian Avant-gardism loosely clustered around a literary and artistic group whose innovations had prompted Breton's comment that "the center of the world has moved to Bucharest." In 1940, together with a group of surrealists that included Paul Păun and Virgil Teodorescu, Gellu Naum elaborated the surrealist manifesto, "Critique of Misery," which defined the basic concepts of Romanian Surrealism. While borrowing some of its notes from the earlier Avant-gardist circles centered around such reviews as *75HP*, *Contimporanul, Integral*, or *Unu*,[16] Naum's manifesto also took its dictates directly from Breton, with whose work he was well acquainted from the pre-war Paris days when he was pursuing a doctoral program in philosophy and establishing the close ties with French language and literature that later made him the excellent translator into Romanian of works by Diderot, Stendhal, Victor Hugo, Alexandre Dumas, René Char and Jacques Prévert.

Like Breton, Naum pleads for the quest of that "point of the mind at which," as Breton puts it, "life and death, the real and the imagined, past and future, the communicable and the incommunicable, high and low, cease to be perceived as contradictions."[17] While reflecting in poetic verse the visual discourse of the painter Victor Brauner, Naum's poetry also announces in Breton's fashion the incandescent itinerary of the poet's spirit engaged in a subversive quest. Sorting and disseminating facts, Naum's approach is to de-familiarize and excommunicate objects by giving them estranged shapes and never tested properties because, as he puts it years later in *Zenobia*, "exactly what you know prevents you from knowing" (71).[18] Echoing the Romanian Avant-gardism's calls for the annihilation of reason, logic, causality, coherence, tradition, proportion, sense and consequence, Naum's poetry seems conceived, in accordance with Benjamin Fondane's advise, as "an autonomous universe, with arbitrary laws and unforeseen hazard. A kind of Morse code."[19]

Particularly significant for this discussion is Naum's poem "Athanor," where he uses the athanor, the bowl on which alchemists rely for miraculously mutating other elements, as a metaphor for the writer/poet searching for a new direction of artistic creation by making new alliances with the sciences, modern mathematics, biology, physics and so on. Naum's preoccupation with the athanor, which also brings to mind Brauner's home in Varengeville that the painter baptized Athanor in celebration of that famed alchemist vessel, echoes Breton's own preoccupation with alchemist projects that marks his surrealist trajectory. In one of the unforgettable moments spent with Nadja, who sees the city lights transformed into a flaming hand, Breton saw fire as the alchemist saw it, that is as the principle of an essential ambiguity whose ordering role is to unite matter with spirit and vice with virtue in demonic sexuality. Like Brauner (who kept notes of his readings of Corneille Agrippa's writings *La philosophie occulte* and la *Magie* and produced the series of paintings Les Chimères, in which he renders spectral presences that bridge the real and the fantastic) and like Breton (who proclaimed his admiration for Brauner's depiction of demons and chimeras as visual representations of the occult), Naum too takes his notes from the writers of the occult, Meister Echkart, Jacob Boehme, and Cornelius Agrippa to show what a fascinating landscape of new projections can be seen through alchemist thinking. If in the alchemist's dream the Athanor was essentially meant to hold and purify matter through long and repeated burning, in Naum's view the mixing of the elements enables the poet to gain access through repeated sensations to a world of sudden parallels, shocking coincidences and seemingly inexplicable connections (Breton's "*hasard objéctif*") that would make one see the field of forces within the world but also outside it. Engaged in a spiritual quest, Naum dives into the unconscious not to decipher the mysteries of the unknown but to explore them, since they represent, as they do for Brauner and Breton, a possible point of contact with a primordial level of consciousness in which will and reason exercise no influence.

But although it draws its essence from Breton's belief expressed in *Nadja* that "all the beyond is in life," Naum's exploration comes not with a breaking of the barrier separating the immediacy of experience from the womb of the unconscious but, as in the case of Romanian Avant-gardists, in the form of a continuum between the rational and the irrational, between dreams and reality, a view that had been in theory suggested in Breton's metaphor of the two urns connected to each other by what might be called a psychic capillary action.[20] Ultimately, Naum's fundamental surreal, which contains rather than conveys meaning, is somewhat related to Magritte's paintings: a world of extraordinary precision suddenly becomes enigmatic by a little secret intervention that is, as Naum puts it, "like a hidden bomb with thousands of detonators within everything the author says, even in the most benign of his affirmations."[21]

Simultaneously an heir to the Avant-gardists and an innovative artist whose talent expands beyond their aegis and Tzara's "acrobatic cries" and notorious eccentricity,[22] Naum insolently trespasses the spaces of objective reality and develops in his fiction a new language by inscribing into it the sensations that seek to undermine words, concepts, actions, and everything that had to do with the old rhetoric. Following the Avant-gardists' reporting of events through a collage principle of disparate views in a process much more intense than the one used by Breton, Naum constructs in his texts a dynamic constellation of news reports and newspaper clippings, a collage structure that re-tailors ready-made reality and generates a new intuition of authenticity in fiction.

As in Breton's case, where a close reading of *Nadja* is necessary in order to assess the full extent of Breton's surrealist project, a detailed analysis of *Zenobia* is an obligatory step toward understanding it as Naum's response and reaction to the Romanian Avant-gardists, especially Brauner, and to Breton. And even though the discussion of *Nadja*'s and *Zenobia*'s similar narrative techniques and textual poetics that I undertake is an important step in this comparative study, my goal is to bring into relief not only Naum's recuperation of Breton's Surrealist objectives, but also the impact Romanian Avant-gardism has had on an imaginative plane in Naum's own work. Skillfully embedded in *Zenobia*, the echoes of Breton's *Nadja* and of Romanian Avant-gardism may reveal not only Naum's appropriations, but also, coming full circle in Naum's work, the significant contributions of Romanian modern fiction to the Surrealist experiment.

Originally published in 1928, *Nadja* is the first and perhaps best surrealist romance ever written. Divided into two parts, a long

Preamble of about seventy pages, which is a kind of illustrated essay on Surrealism, and the shorter, strange story of the encounters with the character Nadja, Breton's book identifies Surrealism's preoccupations, principles, and attitude toward everyday life while exploring notions of love and physical passion. In recounting Breton's love affair with Nadja, a mentally disturbed young woman in Paris, this autobiographical novel (the opening sentence is a question *Qui suis-je*? "Who am I?") focuses on the writer's own beliefs that surreal states of consciousness were best attainable through encounters with the feminine side of masculinity and sexual love.

With her inability to distinguish between illusion and reality, obsessive behavior, and dark eccentricity, Nadja is "*une étoile au Coeur même du fini*," who synthesizes the surrealist trait of the irrational feminine forces that Breton views as complementary to the rational masculine. Although initially attracted to Nadja particularly because she embodies the extralogical and extra rational modes of thought the Surrealists cherished (the first syllable of her name means "hope" in Russian), Breton ultimately abandons her upon discovering her growing madness – Nadja's inability to break the barrier separating sanity from insanity eventually leads to the young woman's institutionalization. The novel ends on a note of exalted hope after the writer's presumable encounter with another woman, whose presence announces "THE DAWN" of a new relationship and whom the first person writer-narrator-protagonist celebrates in the highest degree:

> You who do so wonderfully all that you do and whose splendid reasons, not bounded for me in unreason, dazzle and all inexorably as thunderbolts. You, the most vital of beings, who seem to have been put in my path only so I may feel in all its rigor the strength of what is not felt in you. You who know evil only by hearsay. You, indeed, ideally beautiful. (157)[23]

Eventually, such exalted praise of "supreme love" leads to Breton's mythic view of women expressed in his last prose narrative, *Arcane 17* (1944), which asserts that women might serve as a means for humanity to attain spiritual enlightenment and renewal.

Naum must have read *Nadja* as a form of mental rewriting, in the fashion of Henry James's famous theory that discusses his own meta-view of the creative problems he encounters in the novel he is currently reading and thus trying to solve (or express), and then imagining the ways in which he himself would have dealt with these problems structurally.[24] In a similar fashion, the construction of *Zenobia* must have unconsciously drawn from what Ralph Waldo Emerson, in speaking of "the secret of the reader's joy in literary genius and the contagious character of felicitous expression," defined as "the mechanics of inspiration by which a text induces an independently creative state of mind in the reader, [and becomes] a mechanical help to the fancy and the imagination that trigger in the reader a desire to write."[25]

Published a little over half a century later than *Nadja*, *Zenobia* subscribes to Breton's view of interchangeability of dream and reality and the interference of the conscious (rationality) and the unconscious or subconscious (an antithesis to reality) as two apparently contradictory states that will be resolved into a sort of absolute reality, or surreality.

Both *Nadja* and *Zenobia* detail their author-narrator-protagonist pursuit of and engagement with an ideal feminine counterpart to the masculine side to satisfy the Platonic idea of the original androgynous couple, as expressed by Aristophanes in *The Symposium*. Through catalytic love, this missing feminine part that will be recognized instantly will then dissolve in complete physical and spiritual sameness with the masculine side. Together they attain and nourish an extraordinary kind of perception that erodes and transcends the habitual experience of concrete reality opening up a fluid world of physical objects and imagination that will enable them to reach and experience a different, surreal realm. To implement such textual objectives, both authors use an abundance of signs, words, names, free associations and fantasies of a poetic domain that ceases to give routine directions in a familiar world, but instead creates new affinities or asserts their mystery.

Zenobia, which proposes from the start an unlikely space of indeterminate temporal progression, begins with the narrator-protagonist's visit at the house of Mr. Sima, a neighbor and friend of the marsh-dwelling narrator. Here the dreamlike scenario, alternating between magical reality and hallucination is further complicated when the narrator finds a very weird looking old man named Dragoş, who appears to be asleep on top of a table, and two young men, Jason and Peter, clustered around a beautiful, nameless girl. Wrapped in a dirty sheet of plastic, she had been found "almost unconscious" in the marsh by the two young men whose attitudes and behaviors toward her could not have been more different: Jason, who kicks her and calls her "scum," and Peter, who claims to love the girl madly but appears strangely impotent in his affection. Smitten with the girl's unimaginable beauty, the narrator, who calls himself by his real name, Naum, and who is, like Breton in *Nadja*, the protagonist of his own novel, also falls madly in love with her and begins to speak to her:

> "My dear," I said then, softly to that girl, "because I don't know your name I will call you Zenobia, and you should know that I love you so unimaginably much." (4)

Mr. Sima's remark that the girl is looking at the narrator "as if he were her long-awaited bridegroom," brings into immediate reality the narrator's own account of a dream in which he had in fact met the same girl. Since the dream reveals that the narrator and the girl, who had been the bride of a friend of the narrator's in the dream, have long been acquainted with each other – she is clearly the long anticipated woman of a lifetime quest instantly recognized. In spite of Peter's deep sorrow, the narrator takes her away, to his damp hollow of the dam, where they live together "lying shoulder to shoulder, with our faces pressed against the wet dirt," as they "clutch each other in the darkness" (9). Their passionate love-making continues in their next dwelling, a hollow in a tree, where they "hibernate" during the winter that "is especially harsh in their swamps" (10). Surrounded by lots of snow, during the blizzards, the two lovers live "like moles", telling each other incessantly how unimaginably much they are in love as "the dirt and the dried branches in their hollow rustle faintly" (11). Even on those rare outings away from the hole when they run in the field to stretch their limbs, they never part because Zenobia is permanently attached to her lover's shoulder.

In surrealist manner, Naum's chance encounter with the girl whose real name, as in Nadja's case, nobody knows, is similar to Breton's haphazard meeting with Nadja during an aimless stroll, and it provokes a similar state of emotional upheaval in Naum, the narrator-protagonist of *Zenobia*. Furthermore, the exploration of sexual passion by explicitly recounting the narrator-protagonist's love for Zenobia extends beyond Breton's intense erotic pursuits and occasional illuminations into the occult in *Nadja*. Taking its initial notes from Breton's dictates, Naum's prolonged and richly detailed sexual experiment brings the narration into surreality. In such moments, the narrator describes the feeling as if he were "...falling, without shoulders of wings, in a void without sounds of landscapes. I lived in a state of non-existence, a collapse into the void, from which I didn't want to escape" (102).

An "espirit nouveau" similar to Nadja, Zenobia is as necessary as Nadja was for inducing a systematic disordering of all senses and surreal moments in her lover. Like Nadja, whose response, "On ne m'atteint pas," to Breton's attempts to solve the mystery of her identity, suggests her mysterious, in-between space, Zenobia speaks and acts in dimly discernable gestures that transcend familiar surroundings. Afraid whenever she hears the smallest sound and able to hear the movement of shadows along the walls, Zenobia's actions point not only toward indeterminacy, but also to the existence of a mysterious realm in which virtual realities nearly eclipse actual environments. Her "crystal silhouette" (26) and her continuing whispers "with her lover's shoulders, with his mouth, with his knees" (10), for she very seldom speaks directly to him, suggest her other-worldly quality, and her "chirping about some much more powerful circles that our minds can't do anything about" integrate the novel's magical and material spheres.

Created from the bringing together of two realms, water and earth, the marshes are a hybrid, surreal space that seems to give birth to the unworldly beautiful Zenobia. This Surrealist necessity of bringing together two distinctly different domains to form the surreal is ever present in *Nadja*, not only in the heroine's emblematic drawings ("*Le rêve du chat*," for instance, depicting the cat suspended between the air, where he tries to lift himself, and the earth to which it is bound), but also in the author's own comments about himself. When he states that "in that game which consists of finding a resemblance with some animal, people usually agree that that I am a dolphin," Breton publicizes his condition: like the dolphin, a creature apart from other because he needs both air and water to live, the narrator-protagonist is actively engaged in a search to find surreality, the domain resulting from the merging of reality and unreality. In similarly thinly disguised fashion, Naum's claim from the very beginning that he lives in a crevasse in the "slippery mess" of the marshes whose mud is "all over his cotton socks," alludes to both his being in a space of factual uncertainty and his estrangement from the existing order.

Although Naum does not include in his text cryptic drawings like "The Lover's Flower" or many others that Breton attributes to Nadja, he talks about Zenobia drawing while blindfolded, in the dark, without using her hands and eyes. But even though indebted to Breton's account of his own portrait and Nadja's, and of the curious cut out of a woman's face and hand drawn by Nadja, Naum's detailed description of Zenobia's quasi-hallucinatory drawing of the two of them originates in the concept of *pictopoezie* (pictopoetry) formulated by Ilarie Voronca and Victor Brauner, two luminaries of the Romanian historical Avant-garde. Articulated in the 1924 issue of the surrealist review *75HP*, *pictopoezia* proposed that the link between the imagination and the imagined be erased, camouflaged from view in the communication between the interior subjective and the exterior objective universe expressed in the intersection of the literary and visual arts: "Pictopoetry is not painting/Pictopoetry is not poetry/Pictopoetry is pictopoetry."

In an interesting reversal from Breton, for whom Nadja's unstoppable imagination carries the risk of sinking into madness, and perhaps mindful of Breton's implicit warning in *Nadja* that the surreal world can at any time turn into a deadly trap for the unprepared, Naum devises a reconfiguration of the feminine and masculine identities, reserving for himself the irrational tendencies and endowing Zenobia's character with rational force. Asked during an interview if *Zenobia* is his literary response to Breton's *Nadja*, Naum acknowledged the relationship and then added that in his work the narrator takes over Nadja's role and simultaneously relies on Zenobia to steer him away from madness and despair.[26]

From the moment when the narrator meets her, Zenobia's transparent plastic sheet cover gives a totally different sense of mystery than Nadja's heavy makeup, unfinished around the eyes, her hairstyle, hat, silk stockings and provocative allure. The two heroines' behavior, too, is vastly different. Nadja is a "wandering soul," unaccountable to herself as to others, while Zenobia is peaceful and constant in her love. Later on, after the departure from the marshes and the tree hollow, she begins to work in a "sordid novelty shop" in the city, where her "cutting and pasting letters and flowers on rags and pieces of cardboard" (92) shows none of Nadja's siren-like qualities.

If as a sphinx-type Nadja poses a threat to others and even to herself especially during her hallucinatory phases, forcing the narrator protagonist to abandon her for fear that her frightening inconsistency and unpredictability may harm his own sanity, Zenobia is the narrator's ideal feminine counterpart. Enveloped in what he calls "the axiom of our love," Naum claims to feel Zenobia "so attached, so incorporated in me that I almost didn't see her anymore, just as you don't see your retina" (92). In this deep, obsessive union in which the dualities of self and other vanish leaving the lovers in a downward transcendence into the body, the lovers' physical transcendence leads to an abolition of the quotidian or relational consciousness, with Zenobia acting the part of the valorized half who partakes of, and hence reflects, the adventures of the spirit from one level (or "circle," as Zenobia mysteriously calls them) to the next. Her encoded drawing, "The State of the World," which begins "in the lower part with a multitude of cripples who squirmed in the large box of the malady of the conscious and ended at the top of the pyramid, under a star, where there was no one left" (105), indicates Zenobia's awareness of the disastrous, systematic rituals of purification that the conscious inflicts regularly upon the surreal world of the subconscious. In her pivotal position as a figure imbued with a cosmically mysterious dimension and responsible for the narrator's cycles of transformation, she realizes that the secular city is a place where people cannot imagine transcendence of any kind. Incapable of transcendence, they are bound within a large box of relational consciousness, as incapable of physical love as of mystical experience, which can be reached through the kind of physical transcendence that she shares with Naum.

Thus although Nadja's visions extend beyond immediate experience to countless accounts of a world of weird analogies, strange encounters, and predictions, such as her feeling akin to figures of the past like Melusine, a siren and fairy, or Madame de Chevreuse, a prominent figure before and during the Fronde, her illuminations and insights into mysterious powers do not have the strength of what appears to be Zenobia's permanent ties with, and attachment to, the surreal realm from which she has emerged. Finally, if in Nadja one can discern a female spirit occasionally transforming a male's musings as he strolled around Paris, in Naum's text Zenobia's gentle presence and delicate powers seep their magic over the real world.

Even connecting links between the two heroines turn into significant contrasts as overt references to their spiritual powers result into completely different possibilities. Water images, for instance, which are frequently associated with a female sensibility and which circulate through both novels, are more positive in *Zenobia* than in *Nadja*. As Nadja, in front of a fountain whose jet she is watching with Breton, imagines the waters to be "your thoughts and mine...falling back only to be driven back up with the same strength" (86), she stirs in Breton the shock of recognition at having verbalized the same thoughts he had finished reading about in a vignette preceding the third of Berkeley's *Dialogues between Hylas and Philonous*, in the 1750 edition, where it is accompanied by the legend "*Urget aquas vis sersum eadem, flectit que deorsum.*" Although Nadja's thoughts about the water are of great significance to Breton as they exemplify his own theories of the communicating vases, the water is clearly associated here not with Nadja but with the currents of tradition and cultural intertwining that Breton's text navigates. By contrast, Naum's association of Zenobia with the marshes and the waters from where she emerges, nameless and wrapped in dirty plastic, symbolizes her womanly heritage, the life of birthing and nursing that enables the flesh and spirit to survive, and the female stream that Zenobia portrays and protects as a benevolent priestess grounded in the domestic. Her emotional warmth appears to be the slippery handles that Naum needs to grasp in order to deepen his image seeking sensibility and to destabilize realist scenarios in the loose narrative of the text.

In this context, Zenobia may be seen as not only significantly different from Nadja, but mainly as Naum's personal synthesis of Brauner's watercolors produced during a lifetime, from 1918 to 1965, and ranging from the early "Peisaj cu copaci" (*Landscape with Trees*, 1918/1919), an impressionist landscape in the manner of Cezanne painted when Brauner was an art student in Bucharest, to Brauner's last paintings like "*Dedoublement Vegetal*" (1955) and "*La coupe d'amour*" (1965). The motif of the feminine double, which was present throughout Brauner's work, is duplicated in Naum's novel, whose publication date, in 1985, also marks a sort of corollary of the writer's activity began in the 1930s when he first met Brauner. In both Brauner's paintings and *Zenobia* there is another constant of the two artists' vision: the vegetal world of trees and plants displayed (or captured) in a metamorphic relationship with humans. In "Landscape with trees," trees appear as human subjects in a landscape immersed in the muddy paint of the artist's unconscious suggested in a gloomy background. In the highly conscious titling of "*Dedoublement*" the mature artist is fully in command of his symbolic universe, and paints accordingly. The perfectly divided human figure surrounded by decorative flowers and plants is completely flat, like a poster. The double figure, which hides nothing, is a conscious illustration reminiscent of Romanian folk art and its highly decorative motifs. "*La coupe d'amour*" highlights the wholeness of an intertwined couple, a man and a woman whose closeness seems a refuge from the hostility of the outside world. Closely paralleling these paintings, Naum's portrayal of *Zenobia*'s author-narrator-protagonist who lives in the crevasses in the marshes and in the hollow of a tree where he also makes a home for himself and Zenobia, who is in every aspect his double and who eventually finds work in a shop where she cuts and pastes flowery designs on rags and pieces of cardboard, spans a similar arc of an image rooted in Naum's subconscious (the marshes as a hybrid, surreal space bringing together water and earth) and Romanian folk art which is, in many ways, an homage to the country's flora and abundant forests.

Finally, if Naum makes Zenobia the *sine qua non* of his artistic inspiration, the feminine double who, as in Brauner's paintings enables the artist to accede to an ever higher reality, Breton turns Nadja's pursuits of enigmas and revelations into a sinister endeavor. While Zenobia moves and deepens Naum's imagination not so much as an object of carnal temptation but rather as a power that stimulates his expansion of consciousness, Nadja appears as a solitary figure, a satanic and self-sufficient angel aspiring to an infinite series of metamorphoses. Living temporarily at the Sphinx Hotel, she possesses the dual nature of the monster, revealed to Breton, before their first meeting, by an image representing on one side an angel, on the other a tiger. During walks with Breton, she wonders what role she would have played at the time of Marie-Antoinette; she appears as a *voyante* who sees the city lights transformed into a flaming hand and senses during a walk with Breton that a key episode of *Poisson soluble* took place at a specific spot; and she ultimately becomes for Breton something of a witch closely associated with the devil, as evidenced in her drawing "The Devil's Salute" and in "assuming with an astonishing facility the arrogance of the Devil [when] she has thrown a fold of her cape back over her shoulder" (102).

As Xavière Gauthier points out in *Surréalisme and sexualité*, Breton's views concerning women and the entire surrealist project are in fact determined by a fundamental contradiction within the general surrealist vision of femininity. Contained within Breton's simultaneous exaltation of the supreme lover and his pleas for the unleashing of a completely unimpeded sexuality, such contradiction leads to both the sanctification of woman and to fear and debasement of her. While considering the opposites and extremes that color the portrayal of Nadja, Gauthier comments that Breton sees her as "edible, but she devours men; she is angel and demon, fairy and sorceress, salvation and damnation, symbol of purity as well as sin; she is singular and multiple, repose and turbulence, victim and executioner, nurturance and destruction, protector and protected, giver of life and of death, mother and child, heaven and earth, vice and virtue, hope and despair, God and Satan."[27]

Unlike Breton's vision, Naum's predominant tendency with respect to Zenobia is toward sanctification, an attitude that seems to grow out of his insistence on the cult of supreme, monogamous love. Thus Naum's love for Zenobia acquires something of a mystical or divine quality, closer to Breton's view of woman in *Arcane 17*. As the satisfaction of a lifetime quest, it is an ultimate experience; their complete physical and spiritual likeness leads to their being able to find each other in a specific movie theatre of a big city like Bucharest, based on the vague indication which Zenobia leaves for Naum that she expects him to join her at the movies because she has bought tickets.

Breton's experience with Nadja, which, as Michel Beajour notes, "ultimately *fails* in that he cannot love or truly understand her,"[28] requires further examination, particularly since such an exploration can highlight the differences between Breton's and Naum's ultimate objectives. From the beginning of their relationship, Nadja is not reassuringly reflective of Breton; instead, she goes off into new modes of "different" behavior clearly not prescribed by the masculine norm. Whereas Zenobia blends into Naum body and soul as his missing half of the reconstituted androgyne, Nadja becomes quite literally incomprehensible, and therefore "mad".

The moment of Nadja's final estrangement from Breton, as Bethany Ladimer remarks in her interesting discussion of *Nadja*, is rarely mentioned by critics of the work precisely because this dramatic occurrence in the plot yields the remaining information needed to elucidate Breton's attitude toward her, and toward her madness.[29] The dramatic point occurs when Nadja, while describing a violent event from her past, provokes Breton's own violent revulsion to the account, thus setting the tone for the demise of their relationship:

> I had a frightfully violent reaction to the excessively detailed account she gave of certain scenes from her past, and I judged, perhaps with too much detachment, that her dignity must have been impaired by these events. One story about a blow she had received directly in the face, so that she bled profusely, one day in a room in the Brasserie Zimmer, a story of a blow she received from a man whose propositions she had refused with calculated satisfaction simply because he was despicable (and several times she had called for help but had nonetheless taken the time, before disappearing, to bloody his clothes) this story very nearly, in the early afternoon of 13 October, alienated me from her forever. I do not know what absolutely

> irremediable feeling her derisive, sardonic account of this horrible adventure awakened within me, but I cried for a long time after hearing it, in a way I did not suspect I could still cry. (113-14)

Nadja has become in this account "unrecognizable" in terms of traditional sex-roles definitions, and hence mad in the terms Breton outlines in the passage above. In the light of Gauthier's discussion, Breton's internally contradictory view of women, the reader's interpretation of both Nadja's account and of its reception by Breton may simply communicate the specifically female experience in society. It is an experience that falls under the category of "sex-alienation," and it is closely related to Shoshana Felman's summary of masculine/social suppression of female "difference," because it threatens to prevent a man from finding in a woman his specular and harmonious "missing half," or "Other."[30]

At this point, it is quite obvious that I am aiming here at a restatement of the Platonic ideal of the reconstituted Androgyne mentioned earlier as an essential part of Breton's concept of love. The failure of his love affair with Nadja results, in final analysis, from her failure to conform and submit to this specular or traditional definition of femininity: her madness becomes a hyperbole of feminine difference which Breton finds unacceptable.

In contrast, Zenobia is Naum's complementary half, or as he puts it, "the witness and judge of my existence" (168). Blending the real and the surreal, dream and reality, her plastic wrapping reveals as much as it shadows life while capturing the narrator's hypnotic stance. In the tree hollow and the crevasse in the marshes, she makes possible Naum's reveling in intense experiences of the senses that his spirit was seeking in the city, even before meeting Zenobia.

Here, in the city that sublimates reality in Surrealist manner, the narrator's simultaneously intensely alive and unexpectedly dreamlike drifting turned reality into a realm outside contingency, into a space where reason and unconscious interact:

> After the serene wandering in the daytime, I was tempted by requital: a strange lucidity made me feel the soft floating of the earth with all that was on it. I feared that I would become detached, that I would fall up or down (it was the same thing). I tried to keep as close as possible to trees, lampposts, metal fences, or anything else that I could grab if need be. (95)

Although it detaches itself from a clear origin in the material world, the narrative of the city, which incorporates six of the book's seven chapters, features early on the high-rise building on Mosilor Way (where the narrator used to live before meeting Zenobia) and draws on the image of the corridor as an important recurring narrative symbol. Used as in Eliot's *Gerontion* to suggest the corridor of life discerned rather than experienced, the image of the corridor, in Naum's vision, moves toward a different direction and springs from a different evolving logic than Eliot's. Introduced in the book's second chapter – "about that time I lived alone for a while on a rather long corridor that I would only run and never walk through, a dark and solid corridor on the highest floor of a high rise building" (63) – the image of the corridor's advances the interwoven representation of the real and surreal worlds perceived as a narrative stream.

For Naum, writing about the city is "only reconstitute[ing] the corridor that I used to run through," a corridor having "at one end the visions [that] liquefy you and at the other you go to buy eggplant and so on," and in the middle "a filter zone and through it passes only what by nature can pass regardless of receptiveness or conscious criteria, a hard zone that can be penetrated only by what is destined to become conveyable, a zone whose wild perfection is surpassed only by the necessity (which is equally wild) of remaining in it for a while" (69). Thus if *Gerontion*'s monologue, made up of the thoughts "of a dry brain in a dry season," is distanced from experience and builds on the poem's terrified recognition that neither fear nor courage can save us, Naum's chapter ushers in an invitation suggested in its title, "The Corridor," to connect illusion and reality:

> You open a door and there is another one, and then another and another, until the last one, which doesn't even exist, and so on, until you find yourself at the first one, which doesn't even exist, and you take a stroll to old places because what you thought had released you, and really had released you, becomes a trap and brings you back there to finally understand that your last truth is just as illusory as the first one and to remember that you are always walking a fine line. (57)

Throughout this chapter, narrative bridges thinly disguised as personalized accounts erode the demarcation between the life of the imagination and that of the conscious mind and give a clear direction of the modus operandi of the narrator's consciousness. Erasing clear distinctions between the real and the surreal, Naum incorporates in his narrative friends like "Constantin [who] had died…then he looked for me on Leonida Street, he had some business with me (61)"; those like Ioachim, "an academically perfected cog" (90) with whom he "talked about the terrible curses that caused pohetry to crumble into its perfectly set-in-order curses or uttered by other, more experienced monsters" (75); his neighbor on the corridor, "an aging bride who was lying in wait for me, a Viennese lady about forty-two years old" whose name "was approximately" Gerda (65); and young ladies he used to visit, like Maria, the painter, at whose studio Naum "passed decent hours, soliloquiz[ing] about anything at all in front of her, about how bad the world is, about love and freedom" (76).

Included in the narrative of the city and throughout the book are the Dadaist collages that Naum, in a case of interesting cultural transfer, appropriated, amalgamated and transcended into montages that effectively reconceive reality to reach the heightened awareness which collapses the boundaries between rationality and the unconscious, leading to a final perspective from which the reader, as in the case of *The Waste Land*, can see the whole narrative as a substantial unity.

Like the hollow in the tree, crevasses in the marshes, and the corridor on Mosilor Way, the space where the narrator moves later with Zenobia suggests an imagery of connectedness, an in-between realm reinforced once again by the image of the corridor. Suspended somewhere between the earth and the sky, their tiny room is "one of some sort of aerial cages erected in a row on one side of the tall building, connected by a narrow corridor but isolated from the rest of the building, as if they had fallen from the sky" (89). (My emphasis) Conjuring up further images of connectedness, the stairs of the tall building, the long and narrow corridor and the fire escape ladder to the hot tar of the roof overlooking the city, symbolize the unanchored narrator who negotiates personal and out worldly realms.

The narrator's shifts between the different realms are underscored by a temporal disorientation experienced in the narrative primarily through Dragoş, the old man who is brought to the city to live with the couple. As Ion Pop has remarked in a different context speaking about Dragoş in general terms, "this senile child/old man" found lying on a table top in Mr. Sima's house at the very moment when the narrator met Zenobia, "has something of the surrealist languorous stereotype, a projection of the ancestral hypostasis (his name references the legendary founder of the Moldova state) projected from the subconscious, occasionally opening an ironic eye toward the world of the living."[31] Dragoş's traditional clothes, "the peasant shoes made of pigskin, the peasant pants and long linen shirt…his long, yellowish-gray down past his shoulders" (15) make him look as if time has turned backward. His laughing and dancing by "bobbing his head all the time" in the tradition of Romanian folk dancing seem to link the living and dead communities, and his "dreadfully harmless smile" (15) seems to embrace everything as if beyond the earth, from the transcendent dimension of a mythic perspective.

Bridging magically the worlds of the living and the dead while also joining the world of the present to the past, Dragoş's lyrical presence as a demanding and enabling ancestor seems to embody the qualities of a spirit that moves fluidly from one generation to another while taking on the strength of the dead. In this context, Dragoş's culture-saving figure coming from an indeterminate somewhere makes possible the communication of indefinable currents of feeling and the creation of different discursive worlds characteristic of modernist texts. As Dragoş allows for connections with chthonic and ancestral forces and enhances the narrative's ability to join different realms, the fluidity associated with his person accepted as a given, but not explained, and occasionally questioned ("Maybe Dragoş didn't even exist" [94], as the narrator slyly exclaims) grant him an ideal mythic/historical platform and a binary perspective. He is a figure from the ideal order of historical past, yet he is keeping an eye open to watch from time to time the narrator and Zenobia. His detached presence, venturing out of this world and back in, and his character invested with a multitude of overtones that fill the space of the narrative with a ritual cadence are reminiscent of T. S. Eliot's Tiresias, another figure from the ideal order of myth and the real home of history whose binary perspective allows him to observe all characters of *The Waste Land.*

Eliot's note stating that Tiresias, "although a mere spectator and not indeed a character," unites all the characters and that "what Tiresias sees, in fact, is the substance of the poem," gives a better understanding of Dragoş's character. What Eliot is suggesting – that the reader make an effort to perceive all the characters in *The Waste Land* in an equivalent way, from a position inside the modern world where they are distinct and separate, but also from the Tiresian or mythic position, where the characters melt into each other – is also what Naum attempts in *Zenobia* through the intercession of Dragoş. Like Tiresias, who does not "see" in a literal sense because he is blind (although he "sees" in some suprasensory mode that is the gift of Zeus), but who perceives the contemporary world in the poem from a perspective outside space and time altogether, Dragoş, who keeps his eyes closed most of the time and only occasionally opens one eye, seems to suggest that the reader of *Zenobia* must see the contemporary world of the narrative from the perspective of the Absolute perceived as an inventory of experiences,[32] or at least from a more comprehensible perspective from which past and present seen as linear time is irrelevant. Like Tiresias, a figure from myth, not in time at all, even though he can interact with those who are time-bound, Dragoş's omnipresent character and "his vast experience moving in the bright darkness of the mind buried in itself, like a tradition" (15-16), echoes all-inclusive ancestral voices making possible Naum's surrealist vision. If Tiresias defines his condition as "throbbing between two lives," clearly a reference to his periods as male and female but also to his position as a mediator between timeless and time-bound perspectives, Dragoş's own situation is also an "in-between" state. Reminiscent of the ancient past and the world of the dead, but also of the living, his character is trapped in time and injecting into the narrative frequent reminders of his temporal versatility. His ability to watch the narrator and Zenobia an all the other character in Mister Sima's house in the marshes, as well as his association with the child

Empedocle, in whose company Dragos ultimately bids his farewell, conveys the experiencing at the same time of a child-man and present-past experiencing within a single, unitive perception.

As in *The Waste Land*, where Tiresias can receive Mr. Eugenides' proposition, watch the typist and the clerk, and live as man and woman all at once in a dimension where time does not exist, Zenobia's double perspective and transcendent dimension allow for a simultaneous view of the present and the past, the vision of accumulated ages and the freshness of experience embodied in Dragoş's character.

With a critical eye referring backward to the stated purposes of this article as well as forward to Dragoş's binary perspective, Naum's narrative prompts a further investigation of the connections between *Zenobia* and Eliot's poem. Since *The Waste Land* has been translated and published in Romania as early as the 1960s,[33] it is highly probable that Naum was familiar with the poem; or, to put it differently, it is difficult to see how he could not have read the poem that marks the apex of literary modernism, or how he could have missed its influence on the Romanian literary scene altogether.

With its emphasis on metropolitan existence as a realm where arguments are pointless and where purposes do not exist, and where realistic images embedded in hallucinatory and widening flux of events and memories offer a similar type of *real* reality that the Surrealists considered superior to mere appearance, *The Waste Land* must have appealed to Naum's literary sensibility.

In Eliot's manner, and like Breton in *Nadja*, Naum summons the powers of the subconscious to foreground in *Zenobia* a series of apparently unrelated pictures, dramatically and lyrically presented, to give an impression of an intensely modern, intensely literary consciousness which perceives itself to be a chance correlation (Breton's *hasard objéctif*) of varied elements and apparently unrelated impressions leading to a perception, as in *The Waste Land*, of mundane life seen side by side with suggestive myths. Partly because of such fluidity, *The Waste Land*, *Nadja* and *Zenobia* merge people and places and voices, and the recording of events becomes a part of those events themselves, as distinctions between repeated actions and retelling are blurred and narrational discourse becomes a dreamlike rumination.

Like the published *Waste Land*, which reflects Eliot's life-long preoccupation with urban existence and features the ring of city street names and churches, along with the riverside localities mentioned in the Thames daughters passage, *Zenobia* and *Nadja* are filled with an array of metropolitan material – statues, streets, sites, monuments, etc. – easily identifiable to those familiar with Bucharest or Paris. *Nadja* makes use of Parisian landmarks like *The Hotel des Grands Hommes*,

Place du Panthéon, the *Boulevard Bonne-Nouvelle*, the *Boulevard du Strasburg*, the *Porte Saint-Denis*, the *Statue of Etienne Dolet* in the *Place Maubert*, or the *Place Dauphine* which is, according to Breton, "one of the most profoundly secluded places I know, one of the worst wastelands in Paris" (80). (This qualification, it should be noted, is particularly significant in light of a comparative reading, since "*terrain vague*," the French phrase Breton uses for "wastelands," calls to mind Eliot's poem and its space, with the connotation of a surreal, indefinite realm.) In similar fashion to *Nadja*, *Zenobia* is a veritable city guide of Bucharest, filled with street names like Palade, Moşilor, or Xenofopol, and recognizable town squares and buildings like the Roman Piazza and the Lido Hotel.

There are, however, some clear distinctions in the authors' perceptions. For Breton, Paris is a somber setting, a portal into a realm of the rich and strange conducive to attempts to attain the surreal. During nocturnal walks around the places that frighten the two lovers, Breton recites for Nadja Baudelaire's poems in a voice that "terrifies her all over again" (85) and conveys a nightmarish and eerie quality of a Paris haunted by bloodcurdling specters. The urban scenes bear the stamp of the trivial used to set off the terrible, as churches and monuments form terrifying images and "the footsteps of passers by make Nadja shudder" (185). Even the two drunkards who trouble Nadja, particularly one "lugubriously cracking jokes" (83), contribute to a certain insularity of the two lovers and bring into bolder relief the sinister and apocalyptic side of Paris and a sense of impending doom and apocalyptic dimension.

By contrast, for Eliot and Naum the city is a receptacle with streets and millions of people disconnected to one another, a medium of changing relations in which they exist, and which is neither unreal nor depressing. The speaker of the poem (Tiresias or not; it does not matter here) can sometimes hear a pleasant music from the public bar, a music in direct contrast with the typist's gramophone, the Wagnerian lament, "the Shakesperean rag." There is also the "clatter" and "chatter" from inside the pub where "fishermen lounge at noon." In similar manner, for Naum a blacksmith's son-in-law, who plays in a tavern in Bucharest, appears as a Bach in person – "he looked livid, ecstasy had dimmed in his eyes, he was tottering drunk of music" (68). In the city the narrator is busy visiting his mother and sister, chatting with a young woman from the Department of Classical Philology at the University of Bucharest, and so on.

Unlike Breton's Paris, Eliot's and Naum's cities chronicle the urban existence of ghosts who wear well-known features and suggest an aspect of timelessness in the movement of the masses. Like the London of *The Waste Land* bringing together modern traffic jam, seventeenth century scene of English fox hunters, ancient mythic forest where gods and goddesses reside, and the contemporary residence where Sweeney, Mrs. Porter and her daughter "wash their feet in soda water," the streets of Bucharest are filled, with "too many noises, cars, carriages, streetcars, agitated people" (95) where Naum sees "people [who] went back and forth, all of them looked alive, even the dead, they gave me friendly smiles" (93), or "a lot of dead people, I get along pretty well with them" (96).

Like Eliot, who stages the Stetson encounter among white-collared workers surging into the city and who achieves the universalization of Stetson by the reference to Mylae, Naum's reference to Constantin, a man resembling him, who is both dead and alive and who stops him in the streets to tell stories, or to Mr. Sima, his neighbor in the marshes, makes the same points Eliot makes: first, that Stetson and Constantine and Mr. Sima are every man, including the reader and Eliot and Naum, moving from death to life and from remembering to imagining while blurring the boundaries between them; and, second, that all individuals are fictions in a city that holds widening visions whose rationality, not completely grasped, relays the powerful emotions that lurk beneath the surface and a vague awareness of mystical connections. Like Eliot, for whom the human condition and the city are one, Naum focuses on the human dimension, on the modern city as the unifying element of the concentrated pool of barren humanity. If *The Waste Land* brings together London's city imagery with Baudelaire's *fourmillante cité* as a space flickering in and out of space where dream and reality seem to mix, and with Dante's Limbo, *Zenobia* foregrounds a city that "lay in its carpet of dust" (106) bestowing a dream-like quality, a Bucharest whose description is filled with oblique references to Dante and humorous inserts. Paralleling Eliot's paradoxical pairings of the Rhine maidens and the littered Thames, or of Enobadus' description of Cleopatra as a prime example of love for love's sake and the conversation of a bored modern couple, Naum's juxtapositioning of the Orpheus myth with a local fiddler who had recently lost his wife to consumption and is now ready to go look for her in the other realm, or of Dante and Beatrice and the sordid coupling of Lily and Constantin, generates a similar, surrealist irony and establishes the use of myth as a metaphor of the "ideal order" of experience – a metaphor of what Eliot and Naum took to be the deepest layer of human consciousness.[34]

The juxtapositioning of the characters' mytho-dramatic actions, which reveals contemporary and eternal human qualities, serves a summation of montages, a coalescence of significances and signifiers that enable both Eliot and Naum to present the modern world as merely an infinite cluster of complex experiences. In *The Waste Land*, Mr. Eugenides, the clerk and the typist, and all the others are but varying names and voices whose quality shares a common condition: they are fictitious, referential illusions in a sequence of words. The hierarchy of realism, here, ceases to function and ushers in the surreal, which is contingent on transcendence of the relational realm. Mr. Eugenides is "unshaven," a vague minimalistic image; the clerk is young and has a bold stare, but "carbuncular" is the term that specifically describes him in pictorial detail; the typist is even more vague as a presence; she is invisible. Her environment and cast-off clothing – "stockings, slippers, camisoles, and stays" – are presented, but her person emerges only in reference to her hair, when "she smoothes her hair with automatic hand." In similar fashion, Naum's characters change shape, setting, culture from age to age, melt into one another, repeatedly performing ritualistic functions from behind masks that usually betray little of the distinctive face. His women characters from Maria, the domestic type, to the grotesque Mrs. Gerda, identifiable through her Viennese accent and the chamber pot she holds in her right hand and the garlic in her left, or the large, stout matron, with a little pique hat with a brim turned up on one side and hand bangles, are all one woman seen in minimalist details that do not permit the reader to visualize them. Even Zenobia is described without any reference to her face at all and with almost none to her physical appearance. Such minimalist techniques of presentation work against convention of narrative causing characters like Mrs. Gerda, Maria, or the visiting matron, who are all understood to be real and ubiquitous, to become shadowy and not quite real. Like Eliot's merchant, typist and clerk, and all the other characters in *The Waste Land*, Naum's personages are thrown, or scattered into positions on the fringe of perception and concern, and engaged in unstoppably oscillating movements foregrounding without obvious transition the interference of the real and the surreal. (In *Manifestes du Surréalisme*, it should be noted, Breton also talks about the same unseizable quality attributed especially to women.)

As in *The Waste Land*, the erotic encounters related in *Zenobia* point to relations that cannot ground moral action since morality has to be a by-product of other pursuits. The unforgettable seduction scene, humorously related through the eyes of the deceived Constantin, who finds out that Lily co-opts into her amorous program a very young lad, is reminiscent of the erotic encounter in *The Waste Land* between the typist and the carbuncular clerk, an episode that Allen Tate sees as triggering a giant, ironic laugh.[35] Like Eliot, whose ideas on ethics point in part to Baudelaire's belief that all moral philosophy involves a focus on polar opposites such as bad and good, and whose presentation of certain personages – Mr. Eugenides, Sweeney and Mrs. Porter, the typist and clerk – suggests in the guise of variations of the "love" stories that the substance of *The Waste Land* is the moral ambiguity of these oscillating perspectives, Naum reproduces humorously Constantin's "long string of love's great victims, from Orpheus and Eurydice to Atalanta and Milanion, to Daphnis, Iphis, Ceyx and Alcyone, to the wronged Medea, to Ariadne, to Procris and Cephalus, to Hero and Leander, to Phyllis, Pyramus and Thisbe, to all the Juliets, Ophelias, Margaretas, and Kareninas with all their departed kind on the stage or in the books, finally, the entire cohort of those unhappy exemplars who were murdered or who committed suicide because of their love" (133).

But beyond such mockery of romantic visions of love and moral relativism, Naum's text also accommodates another more androgynous interpretation – that the desired realm of eternal love is not only the realm of female fantasy but also of man's emotional need. This is a realm in which all are loved forever, even when they are old, and desire is shared by both sexes, a viewpoint supported by Mrs. Gerda's happy marriage to a much older husband that satisfies both of them. When the narrator sees Mrs. Gerda for the last time, she is going away as if floating in the yellow, semidarkness of the street lighting to meet her husband on a date. As she approaches him, even though he is leaning on a stick with a silver knob, he kisses her gallantly and they quickly disappear arm in arm around the first corner.

By contrast, in *The Waste Land* where, in the philosophical terms announced in the title, the male is a subject and the female is an object, human love never turns out to be a very profitable path. Since health and wholeness require the unity of male and female, of subject and object, the irresolvable dualism of subject and object (and of man and woman) in the center of the poem is inseparable from the triumph of relational consciousness that locks both in closed systems and prevents communion. By "relational consciousness" here I mean version of F. H. Bradley's theory that Eliot embraced, which states that knowing involves immediate, relational and transcendent stages or levels. If the immediate level is conscious and consists largely of feeling (falling in love, hearing noises, etc.), the second stage, that of relational experience is intellectual and sharply dualistic, in that it involves a breaking down of experience into subject and object. Even though Eliot considered that the mind of the poet transcends these disparate experiences, in the treatment of women where his material, clearly transformed into an aesthetic creation by a highly conscious artist, included his own interactions with his seemingly incurable ill wife Vivienne, Eliot maintained a disparate view of subject (male) and object (female). In the myths central to *The Waste Land*, the king falls first into incapacity of guilt, and his land (the feminine counterpart of the king) follows him into bareness and disease. This mythic pattern, which assigns all blame to the male figures, makes the rejuvenation of the female contingent on the death of the male and defines their existence and health as contingent on male potency. In the mythical position of *The Waste Land*, allusions to the same emerging portrait of women as adjuncts to male power or as victims of it, associates females with direct experience and male with reason, faith, or some other method of gaining knowledge. In myth, female closeness and male remoteness form the complementary conditions for both health and knowledge, and in *The Waste Land* such complimentarity does not exist; as in myth, the absence of connection is associated with disease and waste.

Thus *The Waste Land* features a gallery of unhappy women, depleted physically, intellectually and spiritually. Among the contemporary women in the first part of "A Game of Chess," we encounter a woman at the center of a field of hollow surfaces, seated before a mirror at her dressing table and so surrealistically transformed that she cannot be imagined as a person, but rather as a signifier that points away toward literary and mythic figures; a woman who appears to argue with a man, complains of nerves and ennui, and feels isolated, imprisoned in a relationship that forbids communion or transcendence of any kind, and finally the unhappy Lil, a truncated form of Lily, the flower of Easter or "the cruelest month" in the waste land, is absent but pathetically visible – she is thirty-one years of age, has bad (or missing) teeth, has borne five children, has misspent her allowance to fix her teeth, and ruined her health with an abortion.

For Naum, as for Eliot, love can be disastrous – Lily, the woman Constantin loves, is an aging hag who evokes Eliot's Lil and who, through her erotic exploits, points to a general vulgarity; Maria, who allows herself to be wooed into maturity by a boring academic mole, turns into a submissive type of domestic imbecility; and Jenny Pop dies foolishly by throwing herself out of the window in a tragic-comic reaction to unrequited love. But in spite of such failed liaisons and irreversibly ruinous relationships, Naum affirms his love for Zenobia as the transformative power that transports him beyond the vicissitudes of the quotidian.

The original title of "A Game of Chess" was "In the Cage," an image alluding, as Valerie Eliot suggests in her notes to *The Waste Land Facismile*, the Sibyl in the poem's epigraph. Whether caged or bottled, the women in this section of *The Waste Land* are all entrapped, like the Sibyl, enclosed and dangled as decorations or amusements for men. By contrast, while calling the tiny, "six feet long and six feet wide" (89) room he shares with Zenobia "an aerial cage" (89), Naum suggests through the association of the two lovers with the narrowly circumscribed space his complementarity with Zenobia. Transcending relational consciousness, Naum portrays in *Zenobia* the central consciousness of the androgynous man, with a harmoniously coupled masculine and feminine side, something similar to what Virginia Woolf imagined as the "androgynous mind,"[36] whose quest, whatever its specific form, turns to human love for sanctuary.

Attempted through various human activities – mainly literary, historical, anthropological and religious pursuits – Naum's searches are ultimately evaluated in terms of his references to his love for Zenobia, and all the events he encounters/experiences in his role as seeker for meaning, truth, reality, virtue, the good life take their meaning from their relationship to this love, which is the book's central focus.

With a name associated, as Marian Papahagi points out, with both a goddess and life,[37] Zenobia is a new model for out worldly desire, close to the type Naum describes in his earlier work, *Medium* – "a woman waiting for my love, a woman who will objectify all my desires." (My translation) As embodiment of the feminine principle, Zenobia is also a Penelope, who waits for the narrator eternally and unconditionally. When his wanderings come to an end, and when he draws back from the hallucinatory images overcoming him, the narrator returns home where "in front of the hollow [in the tree], Zenobia was sitting quietly on a heap of dry reeds with her hands in her lap. Her hair had turned white from waiting" (192).

Unlike the conclusion of Eliot's poem that sets the arid plain behind and moves to the fringes of a world where androgeny is absent (Tiresias alone is a complete self-contained structure of opposites), *Zenobia*'s mythologizing structure and the heroine's own quasi-chimerical portrayal, as well as the associations of her character with myth and ordinary enchantments, take a vital step away from that condition and move the reader to a world of harmonious reconciliation of the sensuous with the intellectual, pleasure with knowledge, feeling with thought. Naum's love for Zenobia points to that inward renewal that for Naum is associated with the ability "to communicate forgotten truths from some place where my sensitivity could meet the great general sensitivity lost on the way" (70). As the embodiment of the narrator's surreal longings Zenobia generates the type of love which alone allows for the recovery of a traditional (as opposed to secular) understanding of the world perceived as the interference of dream and reality, and as the union of rather than division into subject (male) and object (female). What Eliot once called "a state of enlightened mystification" Naum achieves through his love for Zenobia.

Continuing this line of thought, one might wonder if *Zenobia* is not the world of *The Waste Land* articulated in terms of female spheres of influence and new strategies for negotiating borders between cultures and individuals. In line with Julia Kristeva's terms,[38] if *The Waste Land*, with its symbolic kind of speech, which is allied with the masculine, connects with a patriarchal society and philosophical thought, then *Zenobia*, with its semiotic or hidden, and unconscious form of discourse, relates back to the feminine and the spiritual. And although in both texts female characters possess a shadowy and tentative personality, a multiperspectival, cubistic portrait of women in both waste lands,[39] the two authors' focus is markedly different: Whereas for Eliot, men of myth make possible the immortality of the earth, and not women who merely suffer and merely die, for Naum it is important to reject "the masculinization of the sacred [that] we've been witnessing for thousands of years, unconsciously and impotently" (132), and to locate centrally in the text a feminine presence that makes possible the interference between dream and reality and complements the androgynous man.

In this sense, both Ion Pop, who talks about an arrangement of the text around "the feminine principle" structured around female characters like Maria, Mrs. Gerda, and the giant matron,[40] and Marian Papahagi, who stresses Naum's focus on the giant "Woman Spirit,"[41] suggest an examination of *Zenobia* in terms of female focalization. Naum's own poetic evocations in interconnected monologues appear symbolically planted to address the central position of the feminine character:

> Perhaps it would be fitting to say here that I felt always around me the all-encompassing presence of a feminine principle that, when I tried to define its features, to give it a face, I named the Woman Spirit. But my receptiveness, still immature, succeeded only in creating the image of a giant woman, as big as the world. (97)

Characterized by structures of diffusion and polivocality as "mother of all mothers, ferocious and indifferent, gentle and generous, deaf, primitive, and infinitely superior to my rude masculinity, she protected me, she shielded me, she guided me through the complicated appearance that envelops us like the air we breathe, without being aware of it" (97), Naum's "Woman Spirit" experiences both human and extraterrestrial characteristics. While coming to terms with "the brightness of this intuitive concept" (97) of her "prefigured 'giantism' [that] had become for me a kind of purely spiritual, abstract, fluid, and formless dimension in which immensity and smallness, anomaly and naturalness, promiscuity and splendor coexisted" (99), Naum formulates a discourse that resembles a lucid feminism by partaking of the difference within, or *différence*, which undermines the notion of individual identity. Furthermore, by disrupting the mimetic program of realism in the representation of women, Naum's portrayal of the Woman Spirit appears in line with Christine Buci-Gluksmann's claim that "the metaphor of the feminine rises up as an element in the break with a certain discredited rationality. It does this by designing a new heterogeneity, a new otherness."[42]

It seems as though Naum needs the aid of this giant female body not only to break through realistic tradition but also, and more importantly for my purpose in this chapter, to annihilate and reverse the disruptive female desire that Susan Suleiman sees as central to Surrealism. From a position of female empowerment, then, Naum's Giant Woman Spirit signals the demise of the patriarchal age typified by Eliot's men of myth, heroes and kings who unify the land, and of

Breton's female *clairevoyantes* whom the founder and chief ideologue of Surrealism imagines to passively "accuse themselves of sometimes adorably moral sins"[43] and whose suffering he has appropriated.

Furthermore, whereas for Breton and the surrealists the female presence functions as "the Other" that permits male writers to reach the world of the second reality, the subaltern whose liminal power and wisdom they wish to appropriate, and whereas for Eliot mythic women are never significant sufferers and are never in a position to unify and rejuvenate the land, for Naum the Giant Woman Spirit is the paradigmatic body through which the text is focalized, a central and powerful presence. Using the feminine as a bridge and conduit to the beyond, Naum situates himself more in line with Irigaray's view of the female as "a *sensible transcendental*" coming into being through a very special male, for whom she "would be the mediator and bridge."[44]

Thus unlike *The Waste Land*'s and *Nadja*'s patrilineal form, Zenobia's feminocentric orientation bridges the world of tradition and modernity, of concrete reality and subconscious visions, and it does so by the incorporation of both female and male views into a union that signals the replenishment and integration of Naum's narrative powers. To consider these developments from a feminine perspective suggests that if Eliot fragments the female body in a cubistic portrait, and if Breton commodifies it in surrealist fashion, Naum reconstructs it as a fascinating narrative, with the aid of both those earlier texts, Naum's portrayal of Zenobia's female spiritual guidance and their experiences of surreal union throughout the novel are once again strikingly similar to Irigaray's description in different context of "la mystérique:"

> This is the place where consciousness is no longer master, where, to its extreme confusion, it sinks into a dark night that is also fire and flames. This is the place where "she" – and in some cases he, if he follows her lead – speaks about the dazzling glare which comes from the source of light that has been logically repressed, about "abject" and "Other" flowing out into an embrace of fire that mingles one term into another.[45]

If religion is Eliot's master in *The Waste Land* as the moral point of view automatically generates polarities and contradictions that beg to be resolved by a higher point of view found, according to Eliot, only in religion, and if dark and occult imagery and sensuous desire dominate Breton's sensibility in *Nadja*, Zenobia is Naum's lover leading him beyond consciousness, out of commonplace reality into the "dark night that is also fire and flames," i.e., the surreal space which by no means erases its complementary physical ecstasy. And even though Zenobia and Naum achieve the embrace of fire that mingles one term into another of Irigaray's description, Naum's book does not end on a heavenly note but in the domain of the marshes where Zenobia waits for the narrator, underscoring simultaneously once again the female relation to the mystical, and the surreal mingling of the worlds of concrete reality and of the spirit.

CHAPTER 2

Modernism and the Male World: The Crisis of Masculinity in *The Bed of Procrustes*

"And still they come and go: and this is all I know –
That from the gloom I watch an endless picture-show."
Siegfried Sasoon, "Picture-Show"

Published in 1933, Camil Petrescu's second novel, *The Bed of Procrustes*, is considered his masterpiece. With its highly unconventional style that merges narrative consciousness and traditional dialogue, it offers both an extension of the Proustian novelistic technique and a new modernist fiction in the Romanian literature of the interwar period.[1]

From the start, the author-narrator recommends himself as a simple go-between whose role is to put the readers in direct contact with the novel's characters – two pairs of lovers who narrate their lives either directly or through their disembodied voices echoed in their journals or private correspondences. Thus, although the journal and letter writing are a logical extension of the nineteenth-century novel's implicit promise of intimacy, as representations of consciousness they operate in The *Bed of Procrustes* beyond traditional novelistic depiction by simulating a perfect knowledge of other minds without recourse to speech and by simultaneously appropriating and abandoning the distinction between narrative and dialogue, interiority and exteriority.

The novel's first three chapters contain the letters of a strange Mrs. T. to the nameless narrator, who had previously suggested to her that she should write down her interesting life. The bulk of the book includes the diary of young Fred Vasilscu, a dashing man-about-town, pilot, and wealthy heir to one of the country's greatest fortunes. The narrator encouraged him, too, to put in writing his various exploits as a trendsetter on the party circuit of an elegant 1930s Bucharest and his secret, consuming love for Mrs. T. The novel concludes with "Epilogue I," recounted by Fred Vasilescu, and "Epilogue II," written by the author-narrator, who gives a final account of Fred's death.

Beyond detailing his two-year relationship with Mrs. T. and the subsequent two years, when he continued to love her mostly from a self-imposed distance in spite – or maybe because – of her great love for him, Fred's diary also focuses on a particular afternoon spent in the bedroom of a quasi-prostitute and sometime actress named Emilia Rachitaru. It is here that Fred sees the letters she received from George Demetru Ladima, a journalist and poet friend of Fred, who had committed suicide four months prior to the time when Fred visits Emilia. Feigning indifference for the letters in order to deceive the unsuspecting Emilia, who thinks that she is entertaining her late afternoon lover, Fred is shocked to discover upon reading them Ladima's love for this vulgar and crude woman.

Fred's reading of Ladima's letters allows for side commentaries and insertion of stories that, while occasionally connected to Fred's own life and interactions with Mrs. T., expand primarily on the dead poet's thoughts, feelings, and epistolary accounts of his professional hardships and unwillingness to compromise his journalistic and social idealism in order to adapt to bourgeois (Procustean) conformity and political compromise. The well-synchronized episodes, which merge Ladima's stories told in his letters to Emilia with events Fred remembers and recounts while reading Ladima's letters in Emilia's bedroom, offer an ingeniously constructive narrative.

In modernist fashion, it enacts the parallel actions of the two couples, Fred/Mrs. T. and Ladima/Emilia, and counterpoises them within the shifting terms of compulsory heterosexuality. As *The Bed of Procrustes* makes clear, in the twentieth-century Romanian society women has ultimate importance in the schema of man's gender construction, representing an absolute not only of exchange value, but also of being the ultimate victims of the painful contradictions in the gender system that regulates men and the male world.

In the novel's world, the two women appear to stand poised waiting for the men to separate themselves outside the feminine sphere and outside the women's lot. An especially incisive commentator, Fred appears as the socially empowered voice of a higher patriarchal utterance – so very high that it gives him throughout the narrative concrete and potent leverage over mere women. More importantly, his patriarchy is not just a monolithic mechanism for subordinating the female to the male; it is a web of valences and significations that commands women's surrender while asserting the intense and potent male patriarchal bonds and relations that regard women as subaltern gender. Thus, in the novel's male-centered society, Fred's conception of women's role is integrated within the limits of homosociality, a term Eve Kosofsky Sedgwick designates as "the social bond between persons of the same sex; […] a neologism, obviously formed by analogy with 'homosexual,' and just as obviously meant to be distinguished from 'homosexual' […] applied to such activities as 'male bonding.'"[2]

Filtered through Fred's eyes, Emilia and Mrs. T. are antagonistic types in relation both to their own sexuality and to male homosocial desire (or man's yearning for male bonding). Conducting his analysis of women as a form of male empowerment that concomitantly uncovers most assiduously the bond between the male protagonists, Fred considers Emilia, for instance, "like a tool that conducts electricity badly or gives you the impression of a discharged battery, because it was initially damaged"; with similar condescendence, he finds "Mrs. T. seems full of life, which makes her excessively sexual, even in the gestures that are inertial in other women (like laying a napkin on a small table when writing a letter; watching the tram leave)" [245][3]. In the obligatory conservation of gendered roles and of male ascendancy, Fred's views gravitate in both instances around the woman's sexuality, which is meaningful in the novel chiefly within the context of woman representing symbolic goods between men. In those terms, vulgar femininity on display belongs to Emilia, the would-be actress and occasional prostitute, and reticent femininity is associated with Mrs. T. If the coarse and vulgar Emilia sells her body and has no goals beyond wishing to be distributed in a good role on stage, Mrs. T. is a model of beauty and refinement. Devoting her time to the shop where she works as a high-end interior designer, Mrs. T. feels liberated from patriarchal control and indulges in the thought that her job is the source of her self-reliance and power. "This job," she tells Fred, "is my self-reliance, the money I earn gives me the right to be myself, to buy nice books and things, not to be offended by the landlord and be kept safe from indecent proposals" (185). But such self-empowering thoughts cannot enhance the status of women like Mrs. T. within a prohibitive continuum structure of men-promoting-men. In the novel's male-dominated world, the schema of female sexuality, whether it be that of the virtuous or the whore, requires the banishment of the woman, in an affair between the men in which the woman's role is intensely moralized and her treatment condescending at best.

In contrast with the two women, Fred and Ladima appear closely tied beyond the categorization of "patriarchy" as mechanisms of the enduring inequality of power between women and men. To the narrative schism within femininity itself that Emilia and Mrs. T. represent, Fred and Ladima appear as malleable and transitive bodies and sensibilities, mutating into both passive and active roles and an elaborate doubling and reversal of identities. Even though Fred has known Ladima only for the four years prior to the narrative present, their encounters during that period touch on the salient points of their entire lives. Further, no matter how different Ladima's reclusive spirit may appear next to Fred's mundane pursuits, such differences are predicated on fundamental similarities. For even though Fred is highly social, a loyal friend and ardent conversationalist who commands devoted friendships, those who know him well recognize his essential solitariness because of "some loyalty and delicacy, a sort of sincerity of life (56)" that also define Ladima's character.

In reading Ladima's letters while simultaneously listening to Emilia's stories, Fred discovers that he shares with the dead poet a symmetrical articulation of man's dependence on patriarchal heterosexuality as a sensitive register for making intelligible the play of desire and self-identification by which men negotiate their social and gender identity – an aspect Fred addresses unequivocally when he states that "for about two years now I've been feeling the need to always be seen with one woman or another" (79).

Concerning such issues, Emilia's interventions, which are inserted between the readings to provide additional information or clarify the content of Ladima's letters, serve two important purposes. First, they make warranted and explicit Ladima's jealousy and his threatened masculinity caused by his accurate perceptions of her numerous betrayals. Second, through Fred's perception of an alarming scarcity of love that Emilia can offer, they reveal indirectly both the mechanisms by which gender inequality is structured and the leap from the relation of heterosexual to male homosocial bonds. Specifically, since Emilia's sexual manipulations are her primary strategy for economic survival, Fred insinuates with apparently timeless authority the process by which, in the schema of female sexuality, woman and whore beget each other, taking their shape from the social dictates of gender difference. Further, since Fred visits Emilia to satisfy his natural quota of sexual discharge, sexuality is a highly charged signifier for differentials of power in which women, split between the virginal and the whorish, submit to men within the context of circulation and exchange, prompting them to seek bonds of higher order and substance with other men.

With Fred enacting his double part as an investigative observer of the relationship between Ladima and Emilia and of his own relationship with Mrs. T., the couples' parallel stories draw on the complementary figures of the four lovers while building up a combination of tension and mystery, a "superior detective emotion"4 haunting the lovers' lives and deaths. Ladima commits suicide after learning the truth about Emilia and her sexual dalliances, and, after rejecting all pleas of being reunited with Mrs. T., Fred dies in a plane crash that has all the indications of a possible suicide.

For many years, I took Camil Petrescu at face value. As my analysis demonstrates, I have done straightforward readings of his characters and concentrated almost exclusively on homosociality without picking up on the warnings about missing the obvious with which *The Bed of Procrustes* is shot through in the case of the two male protagonists: Ladima fantastically unable to see that Emilia is a paid escort to wealthy and socially influential men and Fred incredibly unwilling to allow for the comfort of Mrs. T.'s love for him. Since translating this novel, I have come to think that there is room in *The Bed of Procrustes* for discussing not only the dictates of the male protagonists' homosocial bond, but also their ultimate inability or refusal to connect with women as a demonstration of a modernist crisis of masculinity – a crisis both willed and tragic.

Further, if it is true in this novel that both female characters, Emilia and Mrs. T., exist in some meaningful relation to the role of 'lady,' their signifying relation with the two male characters grows more tortuous, adding another Procustean dimension to the men's stories.

Since Mrs. T. is a woman as she is a lady, and since Emilia is a woman not in relation to her own desired role of 'lady,' but only negatively, in a compensatory relation to Mrs. T., what is clear is the centrality of sexuality in the novel and of sex as an especially charged intersection for the exchange of meanings between sexes.

From such a perspective, and keeping in mind even a summary account of the novel's plot, The *Bed of Procrustes* strikingly echoes the efforts of modernists like Ezra Pound and T. S. Eliot to solidify the male's intellectual and sexual anxiety over the "fermenting chaos" or the unruly corporeal, often coded as the feminine. Pound explicitly formulates creativity as "the phallus or spermatozoid charging head-on the female chaos,"[5] while Eliot, somewhat less overtly, complains that Hamlet lacks an "objective correlative" and suffers from "the stuff that the writer could not drag to light."[6] In discussing both Ladima and Fred in their relations to Emilia and Mrs. T., this "stuff" is linked, as I propose to show, to an anxiety and crisis of masculinity (or male hysteria) that found their way in *The Bed of Procrustes* after being drawn from the two favorite sons of literary high modernism, Pound and Eliot, with whom Camil Petrescu was well acquainted from his engagement with the world of theatre and the literati.[7]

Grafted into the narrative much like Eliot's catalogued typology of women in *The Waste Land*,[8] the two women, Emilia and Mrs. T., stand for bad and good, respectively, womanhood. The choice of sexuality as a thematic emphasis for my discussion brings into salient focus at this point the degraded sex scene between Fred and Emilia, on which most of the narrative is centered. Carried out in Emilia's bedroom, this scene, which also functions as the novel's primary setting, is highly reminiscent of the carbuncular clerk and the typist's sordid encounter in the "violet hour" of *The Waste Land.* For although different in form from the poem, *The Bed of Procrustes* dramatizes, as the poem does, the protagonists' experiences of sexual repression projected against an urban, decayed background and complicated by the pairing of unlikely lovers whose stories, feelings, and confessions trigger dislocated desire and sexual anxiety.

The evolution of male hysteria into a pronounced and even commonplace condition coincided with an array of historical and cultural shifts, of which the most well-documented event in undoing social, gender, and sexual categories was the mass destruction of the First World War. Adding to the symptoms of "shell –shock" and of the "war neurotic" Freud articulates in *Beyond the Pleasure Principle*, Sandra Gilbert and Susan Gubar write that "the unmanning terrors of combat lead not just to a generalized sexual anxiety but also to an anger directed specifically against the female."[9] Beyond the mass destruction reverberating with a disintegration or dissociation of body and soul, women appear as emblems of sexuality gone awry. Either as violated ingénues or neurasthenic vamps, women are demonized through mid-century modernism for their newly acquired liberties and targeted for the modern male's wounding, or even castration.

Like Eliot and Pound, who did not participate directly in war, Camil Petrescu was highly conscious of the male body's fragility and its potential resemblance to the female hysteric, replicated outside the trenches as the less easily definable traumas of social angst. His first novel, *Last Night of Love, First Night of War* (1930), dealt primarily with the specter of sexual anxiety, the trauma men exhibit after serving in battle, and their overtly feminine response to shock translated into a crisis of masculinity. Petrescu's second novel, *The Bed of Procrustes*, develops its characters' threatened masculinity by complicating their social and cultural circumstances and affective engagements and by delving further into the mechanisms and paradigms of masculinity in crisis.

Maximizing the veneer of respectability she possesses, Emilia secures Ladima's love by calculatingly lying about her scandalous and publicly-known sexual encounters. Located primarily at the crossroads of Emilia's observations and Fred's readings of Ladima's own letters to Emilia, Ladima's character and sensibility are framed in Fred's consummate narrative. Its calculated cleverness stirs deep compassion for the betrayed and tormented Ladima and contempt for the promiscuous Emilia. Looking in one of Emilia's drawers at a photograph attached to a pile of letters tied with ribbon, Fred talks about Ladima's tall and thin looks,

> with round eyes and large, deep sockets... with a sergeant-major's moustache and a hairdresser's parting, with his black alpaca jacket and white shirt, the collar always too wide, starched, with big round cuffs, like rain pipes, pinned with pink cufflinks onto the shirt, while the other cufflinks were small sticks, of course in gold – who knows what souvenir... He would have had a beautiful head, if he hadn't been so old-fashioned... I don't think he was more than 35-40 years old. (90)

Ladima's happiness is in the first place about Emilia's depravity, i.e., her numerous erotic encounters that divide her ever more from Ladima's purity and devotion. His most piercing emotion seems attached to jealousy and to the subsequent suppression or concealment of sexual desire bound to turn Ladima into a disabled man, split between erotic servitude to Emilia and an incorruptible political and artistic engagement that makes him feared by the establishment (the corrupt political scene of Nae Gheorghidiu and his friend, the wealthy Tănese Vasilescu, Fred's father) and highly respected as a gifted poet and director of the prestigious journal *Veacul* (*The Century*).

Ladima's naiveté regarding Emilia reveals a pattern of refusals, suspending rather than negating the possibility of being duped and producing an unlimited – because undefined – psychological potential, which is far from ascetic, prudish, or transparent. Although he is not, as the literary critics of Communist Romania considered him, the exploited artist destroyed by the pressures of capitalism and material deprivation,[10] Ladima exemplifies a passing away of a certain type of artistic sensibility. His penchant for chivalric posturing (he risks his life to defend Mrs. T. from an insanely jealous Fred), lengthy and passionate letters, and lyrical expression, which once connected an individual with tradition, seem to be facing the endless vertigo of modernity, while his journal writing (an alien usurper of storytelling) is an indication of his sustained effort to cope with the abbreviated nature of modern life. But this gradual atrophy of narrative and lyric form required in an age cut short by the shift to information can only partially justify Ladima's isolation and lack of connection to his social circumstances, especially since he continues to be highly regarded as a poet and feared as a journalist with a poisonous pen.

The profound significance of Ladima's inwardness and of his involvement with Emilia is best captured in Rimbaud's verse that Ladima himself, painfully aware of his condition, writes to Emilia in one of his last letters: "Des serpents géants dévorés par des punaises" (274).[11] As each of Ladima's letters addressed to Emilia that Fred reads is almost always followed by Emilia's vulgar commentary, Ladima's disembodied voice reverberates as that of the ideal poet constructed in Eliot's theory of "dissociation of sensibility" and of a spectral Fisher-King whose sexual anxieties are coincident with Ladima's personal experiences of sexual repression. Focused on journalistic writing and his own poetry, Ladima has only once been involved sexually with Emilia and stubbornly saves their intimacy for a muffled and distant future of married bliss. Further, Ladima's sudden and impervious infatuation with Emilia on the one hand, and his social prominence on the other, reveal Ladima's double personality – a split pointing to the "hysteric" relationship between mind and body that represents a dominant version of the crisis of masculinity in modernism.

According to Eliot, a "dissociation" or split between intellect and emotion, a "disparity between idea and image," reflects a "progressive deterioration of poetry since the thirteenth century."[12] In his essay on Milton, Eliot broods: "In the seventeenth century a dissociation of sensibility set in, from which we have never recovered."[13] Such literary dissociation, which according to Eliot energizes innovation of the modern lyric, explains Ladima's superior creativity, which even his detractors are forced to acknowledge. A prolific and talented poet, Ladima is the very embodiment of what Eliot hails when he proclaims the dissociated subject as the ideal poet: "the more perfect the artist, the more completely separate in him will be the man who suffers and the mind which creates."[14] Inserted in his letters to Emilia, Ladima's verses provide an imaginary space where he articulates his brooding and anxieties over personal experiences. Hinging not upon his erotic desire for Emilia but upon the impossibility of his sexual self-identification through her, Ladima is an off-screen spectator who sees but refuses to accept Emilia's promiscuity while seeking refuge in his regenerative verse. Detaching physical engagement from his consciousness, Ladima forges a hysterical identification with Emilia through a systematic corporeal self-mutilation and passive participation in his own sexual fantasy involving Emilia and their relationship of love.

At the opposite end of the spectrum from Emilia's vulgarity and cheap sexuality, Mrs. T. is the epitome of elegance and grace. Her strong sexual desire and erotic encounters with Fred speak of a woman trapped in the cage of her own passion. But her satisfaction of being understood is tainted because Fred, the man she desperately loves, does not wish to stoop to self-exposure. There is, in Fred's reticence and even in Mrs. T.'s behavior, a certain vacillation between the two lovers' communication with each other and an entrenched cynicism about the dishonesty of social signification. They always meet in remote locations in the country to secure and protect the secrecy of their relationship from Bucharest's high society, in which both of them are highly visible personages. Swinging between a Romantic belief in psychological interiority and a Realist attention to the social significance of a couple, the relationship between Fred and Mrs. T. evinces the characters' conflicted psychological selves that wish to be utterly transparent and yet resent the suggestion that their secrets are legible.

As Mrs. T. cannot ultimately fulfill her lover's fantasy of silent communication and his attempt to reconcile the surface/depth dimension of his life, Fred appears broken and amputated emotionally like someone who both dissects and mutilates his own flesh. His feelings toward Mrs. T. reveal an acute discomfort with her body and a particular resistance to female corporeality that hinge upon his identification with hysteria. More often than not, Fred's reflections on Mrs. T., and especially his fragmented close-ups of Emilia half naked in her room, echo Eliot's portraits of women and the great poet's own discomforts with female corporeality fractured into multiple women in both *The Love Song of J. Alfred Prufrock* and *The Waste Land*. As in the two poems, *The Bed of Procrustes*'s thin plot pivots upon the tropes of sexual anesthesia and castration enacted by both Fred's and Ladima's characters.

While visiting Emilia, Fred acts and comports himself much like Prufrock when he confesses his essential fear and dissociation of women and shows his hysterical symptoms to be both etched upon his body's surface and projected elsewhere: "I've never been married, I haven't even lived with a woman, and any woman that's ever undressed simply, for me, made me hold everything inside, astonished, the way one's breathing is held when waiting for something to happen" (44). Like Prufrock, who is afraid to drown in the sensuality of the alluring mermaids "in the chambers of the sea," Fred is afraid of Mrs. T.'s love even though he spies on her every move while letting his friends mock her for pursuing him. For much like Ladima's repudiation of his sexual needs and his glaring self-deception that perpetuate his excruciating pain, Fred's refusal to accept openly the real object of his desire (whether involving casual sex or particularly the obsession with Mrs. T.), gives the most haunting portrait of the two men's essential loneliness, the longing or "stuff" that they could not fully articulate even to themselves. This "stuff," which even the writer could not drag explicitly to light, schematizes the two male characters' crisis of masculinity, or the male hysteria, which *The Bed of Procrustes* ultimately delineates.

As a modern hysteric, Ladima corresponds to several of the type's characteristics enunciated in Pierre Janet's *Psychological Automatism* (1889) and *Mental State of Hysterics* (1892). According to Janet, the hysteric was a victim of "dissociation of personality" suffering from "mental disaggregation," and "psychic weakness."[15] Whenever Emilia entertains her callers, Ladima plays cards in the room next door with her sister and, whenever Emilia is away from home with one of her many clients, he assumes that she is in her native town of Bazău to oversee family affairs. Even when he has occasional outbursts of jealous rage, Ladima ends up crawling back to Emilia and begging for her forgiveness, thereby showing all the signs of an "unassimilated second self, independent of our known one."[16] By clinging to Emilia's promiscuity as cover for his castration, Ladima acts like a prototypical modern hysteric, whose body is neither fully under the control of consciousness nor entirely accountable by psychological discourse. His dissociated "second self" gravitates in exclusively mechanical ways toward Emilia, whom he sees, in spite of all evidence pointing to the contrary, as an image of innocence and femininity, wronged by critics and jealous colleagues who refuse to admire her great talent as an actress.

Precisely because the possibility of loving a woman like Emilia is socially improbable, Fred is shocked to learn of Ladima's letters to her. As he cringes at Emilia's touches and panics at the thought of being found naked in her room by Emilia's sister, Valeria, whose voice he can hear on the other side of the door, Fred is actually projecting the habitual way in which he always retreats fearfully behind his circumspection from even the most tacit or intimate offers (notably Mrs. T.'s) to bridge the distance between himself and others. As an inactive lover following Emilia's body and movements whenever she hand him the letters or brings him coffee, Fred crafts himself into a disembodied observer enacting on an immediate level Baudelaire's dandy poet/spectator conceived as "a kaleidoscope endowed with consciousness."[17] Akin to Baudelaire's gaze in his paradigmatic poem "To a Red-Haired Beggar Girl," Fred's camera eye objectifies Emilia's female body so that he himself can become what Pound, following Baudelaire, crafts: a spectator that is simultaneously a sexual agent ("enacting the copulation of images" [of Emilia's body]) and a disembodied observer.[18] Impelled by an intoxicating personal identification with Ladima while reading the poet's letters, Fred also offers himself as "a contrasting disembodiment"[19] while lying in Emilia's bed.

Thus, although Fred visits Emilia on a sexual quest, he seems to extend his body through projection and displacement into a state of intense revulsion whenever she touches him. Fred's alienated body, which seems controlled by another master, performs the "dissociation of sensibility" that structures many modernist works and that here, in Fred's case, underscores the male hysteric's paradoxical attraction to and disavowal of the corporeal by enacting the copulation of the juxtaposed images of Emilia's body for Fred as the disembodied observer. Sitting "dryly" on her bed, Fred observes Emilia undressing in silence:

> Her arms stretched, she lifts her coffee-coloured dress over her head, then her chemise, and she remains naked, with a full midriff, with soft and a little smoky skin, only waiting for the body to bend, to become thick lines. Her breasts are held, like those of a dancer in a shell, in the black net cups of her brasserie (nets which remind me of those used by men to hold their hair in place). A blue belt presses a little into her stomach, and from its sides hang the garters that stretch her stockings. Framed between the belt and the two garters which descend on the inside of her thighs, there's a little blond flower on a little flesh cushion, an equilateral triangle because of the width of the young belly, the centre of her woman's magic. This undressing seems unbelievably precise, for me it's like a threshold stepped over, as I know how long the way here can sometimes be, and how uncertain [...] This strong white woman who sensed I like watching a naked woman, undoes her belt at the back, and it comes off with the entire apparatus of wide elastic bands, leaving the body naked, like the back of a young horse

> once its harness is off. The net caps on her breasts also come off. She sees me looking at her and asks surprised, the way you ask someone if they won't sit down, with big dull eyes, like stagnant green waters, "Won't you undress?" She is waiting, thrown on the wide, king size bed, a corner of its green cover aside, after she cautiously put a small towel under the pillow.
> I feel her a stranger in my arms, a separate body, maybe because I am a little obsessed with the thought that her sister in the kitchen may discover the evolution of this visit (although it's certain that's exactly why she won't barge in, that they have an understanding), but also because Emilia lends something programmatic to this fact which, under these circumstances deserves it dictionary name, i.e. it is an "act." (76-7)

Fred's fantasy of impersonating Ladima corresponds to another primary mechanism of hysterics – their capacity for identification. Although Fred sees this identification with the hysterics as their ability to "express in their symptoms not only their own experiences but those of a large number of other people,"[20] more crucially hysteric identification is suggested in *The Bed of Procrustes* in the hypnotism that hysterics exert over other hysterics, and it roughly translates into a hypnotism rooted in the fear of having the same kind of experiences. Memorably, in the novel Fred meets and befriends Ladima when the latter stands up for Fred for insulting Mrs. T. out of a jealous rage that overcomes him when she is in the company of other men to whom she appears to be attracted. Manifested as a tension between interior impulses and exterior control in a situation that places sexuality at its center, Fred's reaction partakes on an immediate level of the valences of the male hysteric. Later on, when Emilia gives Fred Ladima's letters, Fred's reading both elicits and dramatizes projection through permeability, the way "exterior facts are continually transformed into interior elements and psychic events are exteriorized."[21] In this way, the information conveyed from Ladima's letters is not only an accumulation of homosocial desire, but also appears to be continually transformed into Fred's own interiority, which is in turn exteriorized as his own psychic outcome.

Thus, Fred's hypnotic attraction to Ladima's letters is not only an expression of his hysteric capacity for "identification," but also reflects an unconscious tendency to inversion by which Fred fears, on an immediate level, that he too, not unlike Ladima, could be duped by a very stylish and much admired Mrs. T. By projecting his fears and hysteric identification with Ladima while in Emilia's room, Fred is overcome by a state of torpor. Passive and unable to move, he is disaggregated like Eliot's Prufrock, who has been alternately attracted to a montage of "arms, braceleted and white" and taken aback by a compulsive close-up of them "downed with light brown hair."[22] Staging Fred in a situation similar with Prufrock', *The Bed of Procrustes* makes tangible once again the male hysteric's fear of identification with the female body. As Emilia attempts to smile and draw close to him, Fred takes pains to push her back and to create a desired distance from her:

> I smile gratuitously and coldly. She comes near me deceived by my smile and I feel her warm as a meal, her breath too heavy, her face too shiny from perspiration, and when she presses against me her skin is stuck to mine, so that any movement is like skinning. Disgusted, I avoid her attempt to kiss me. (79)

Spurred by the scapegoating of female sexuality, Fred's unconscious tendency to provoke unexpected identifications merges a fragmented Emilia into all women, as in *The Waste Land* in whose note about the "spectator" Tiresias Eliot claims as well that "all the women are one woman." Here is Fred, in Emilia's room, invoking corporeal mutilation and psychic shock caused not only by the woman thrown on the bed, but also by all women:

> I feel like waking up from a chaotic slumber…It feels like the link connecting me to this woman was interrupted and I became amorphous once again. It's all over. The former thought was associated with others, at the same time enhanced with blurring, subconscious plunges which were all designed to get this woman to bed…But now everything gets connected, within me, with smelly leeks; black bruised withered skin. Just like Emilia managed to become unique a moment ago, all women, are now just like the woman downstairs. (206)

Although the invocation of women representing the male characters' anxiety over fleshiness in *The Bed of Procrustes* is limited to Emilia and Mrs. T., who cannot measure up to the female chorus of women in *The Waste Land*, from the Philomel to mad Ophelia, the pub room Lil, or they typist, they are etched into the narrative and, in their own way replicate Eliot's personages. The hyacinth-girl, who elicits and manifests the most sensualized response in *The Waste Land* ("Your arms are full, and your hair wet/I could not speak") and who potentially encapsulates and supersedes her own gender, is, like Mrs. T., the only mediator of male desire present in the poem as in the novel. Precisely because he feels attracted to her, Fred acts out a refusal to acknowledge openly his love for her or to admit his anxiety and insecurity toward a woman like Mrs. T., whose sexual freedom and financial independence secured through her job place her outside the patriarchal realm and Fred's control. Reduced to silence and forbidden to speak to or about Fred, Mrs. T. is also a Philomel. With her tongue symbolically cut out, so that she is "beyond speech," Mrs. T. claims one of the novel's most powerful images that relate to male hysterics' response and reaction to female affection.

Although *The Bed of Procrustes* does not foreground the apocalyptic vision of a female chorus featured in *The Waste Land*, the novel details like the poem wide-angle views of Emilia's bed, body, undergarments, and toiletries – "on her dressing table in front of the mirror..., next to the mascara brush, the tweezers, the shaving machine, the little blush box, a bottle of "Original Coty" and the toilet water, all lined up" (87). Even her behavior is reflective of several of the female characters in Eliot's poem. During the afternoon spent with Fred, Emilia echoes both the hyacinth girl and Maria in *The Waste Land* as "she waves her hand in front of [his] eyes, like chasing a bee, as if she wanted to shred, physically, the canvass of [his] thoughts [before asking the absent minded Fred] 'What are you thinking about?'" (79). Her bed, where she receives her lovers, echo the typist's "divan...(at night her bed) [piled with] stockings, slippers, camisoles, and stays" (CPP 45) catalogued in Eliot's poem. And, from Emilia's own stories, we may infer that her existence and mechanical sexual dalliances are patterned after the typist's modern, single life, which allows for the sex-scene that will unfold with the arrival of her "young man carbuncular" who "assaults" and "encounter(s) no defense." But although Emilia's body canvasses the novel engaged in assaults and surrenders that involve occasional lovers, there is definite suppression of corporeality in her encounters with Ladima. With his shabby clothes and genteel inclinations resistant to the rabble and rubble of the mundane scene, Ladima's passivity evokes a sexual anesthesia reminiscent of the sexual wounding of the Fisher-King, glaring from the narrative in spite of Fred's skillful sexual plot built on Emilia's discredited body. Simultaneously hidden and omnipresent, much like the Fisher-King, Ladima is etched and constructed into the narrative as a castrated and vulnerable phantom. His only flickers of heroism appear consumed in futile encounters with the cultural establishment that lead to further isolation and "hysterical" enervation reverberating with a dissociation or disintegration between Ladima's body and mind.

Fred's desire to enter and configure Ladima's past from the letters addressed to Emilia not only binds him over to the dead poet, but it also recommends him as the primary authority in digging up and interpreting Ladima's life. In the process of this psychic excavation, Fred opens up and embarks upon identifying with Ladima. As if hypnotized by Ladima's ghost while reading the letters, Fred responds hysterically by beginning to inhabit a hybrid consciousness, which blurs the boundary between his own living body and the apparition that is Ladima's ghostly presence: "I smoke, deep in thought. My own life stirs in me, summoning like you summon a spirit, and I suppress it with difficulty and sadness. When Emilia tries to kiss me on the lips even though I never allowed her to do that, I start reading again" (100). Specifically, in the narrative context, as Fred and Ladima meet on shared grounds (Emilia's room) but never identically occupy it (their reactions to her are diametrically opposed), they merge into a familiar version of the modernist double, articulated between the hypnotized body (Fred) and that of the projected and repressed (Ladima).

Sacrificing and then sublimating his own person, Fred's undergoing process of depersonalization takes away the feeling of Fred's own existence. Submitting to this temporary depersonalization and denuded of energy, Fred's body becomes "the body etherized on a table," a condition that, akin to Eliot's "patient" in *The Love Song of J. Alfred Prufrock*, produces his sexual anesthesia and promotes not only his resolute distancing from Mrs. T., but also engenders the in-between zone of his and Ladima's ghost-like bodies. Fred's continued inability to distance himself from identification with Ladima culminates in his radical separation from Mrs. T. and his subsequent suicide, which further enacts, as in Ladima's case, Fred's unsuccessful attempts to control the involuntary reflexes, dissociated bodies, and conditioned corporeality of male hysterics. The undepictable embodiment of both Ladima and Fred as modernism's male hysterics seems to belong to an uninhabitable landscape, a narrative Procrustes's bed that, like Tiresias's domain in *The Waste Land*, cuts into myths of cohesive embodiment and stable gender structures.

While both men's thoughts and emotions are made visible and tactile and their sex lives are deconstructed beyond the scope of male homosocial desire, their "hysterical" masculinity draws us toward the characters as tropes of our own psychological haziness and sexual uncertainties. As the novel's characters urge the reaction of its readers for clues about ourselves, our curiosity about the characters' private lives and sexual crises is really symptomatic of a Procrustean anxiety about the authenticity of our own experiences.

CHAPTER 3

A Feminist Epistemology of Sensibility: Hortensia Papadat-Bengescu's Hallipa Trilogy

"Our concern is with the body."

H.D., Notes on *Thought and Vision*

> It will be enough to remember that the Baroque composers, very much including Bach, practiced a craft of somewhat mysterious and arcane causes and effects, that they used rhetorical figures consciously to invoke specific emotional and moral messages, and that these messages, whether or not they are felt or heard, can be found on the pages of the score.

James R. Gaines, *Evening in The Palace of Reason*

> It is decisive for the fortune of nations and of mankind that one should inaugurate culture in the *right place* – *not* in the soul (as has been the fateful superstition of priests and quasi-priests): the right place is the body, demeanor, diet, physiology: the rest follows.

Nietzsche, The *Twilight of the Idols*

The cultural activism and literary works of Hortensia Papadat-Bengescu remain a remarkable legacy of early twentieth-century Romania, a country where the socio-economic conditions and educational structures combined to disempower women. Engaging in the discourse of defining women's new identity and their role within a patriarchal cultural space, Papadat-Bengescu's Hallipa trilogy – *The Disheveled Maidens* (1926), *A Bach Concert* (1927), and *The Hidden Road* (1928) – uncovers significant social concerns, records the potential disordering of the country's traditional society, and reveals the growing participation and emancipation of women in redefining it.[1]

Fully immersed in the twentieth-century intellectual debate that undermined the Cartesian split between body and mind and in the urgent new agenda in literary modernism occurring in canonical works immediately after the First World War that empowered the representation of the body, the trilogy offers itself as an epic of the body represented in distinctive ways. Defined by their subtle explicitness in the representation of the body, the three novels celebrate the life of the body as a greater reality than the life of the mind and seem configured to illustrate Papadat-Bengescu's preoccupation with the potentiality of a woman's body – a focus that appears poised to heed T. S. Eliot's insistence in his 1921 essay on the Metaphysical poets that when poets ask us to "look into our hearts and write" they are "not looking deep enough… One must look into the cerebral cortex, the nervous system, and the digestive tracts."[2]

Papadat-Bengescu's representation of the body in terms of the politics of the construction of gender and of culture benefit from the pivotal endorsement of the representation of the city in general as the source and space of women's worst vices – sexual indulgence and over consumption. All the novels of the trilogy embrace the city of Bucharest, Romania's capital, as a fashionable new moral and urban geography where women who move away from traditional environments, such as rural or small town surroundings, give in to their sexual passions, and embrace city life to become agents of social change.

Centered on the disintegration of Lenora and Doru Hallipa's marriage (a metaphorical allusion to the collapse of the old patriarchal order and their subsequent move to the city, *The Disheveled Maidens* chronicles the living city with its streets, intracity transport, public buildings, private residences, museums, shops, and the multitude of inhabitants through the voice of Mini, a young woman commentator and occasional character in her own narrative.[3]

The intersections of Mini's double narrative functions provide ample occasion for the portrayal of the socially constructed and morally meaningful female types of the time. From the sexually indulgent Lenora Hallipa, through her promiscuous daughter Mika-Lé and Mini's feminist friend Nory, who wears her hair "cropped short on the nape" (63), makes gender-specific comments, and never misses a chance to promote her socialist views, to the not-so-kind-hearted Doctor Lina, the quiet Elena Hallipa, Lenora's oldest daughter, and the alienated, nameless woman of Bucharest, all the feminine characters bear in some form or another the unmistakable trademarks of the disheveled maidens of the title who find their haven in the city. Ushering in the new age as "girlfriends," some look like "scrawny mannequins [with] dull skin, exaggeratedly large eyes, and lanky, scraggy hands; on their narrow busts, [they have] breasts whose vain attempts at showing off were more salacious than any voluptuous forms" (76).

Out of step with the Romanian cultural assumption of the era, which required that young girls or unmarried women in the outskirts of the city, as well as in towns, villages, or even more rural places, wear their hair braided and tight on their head (*împletite*) as a sign of their virginity, the new and fashionable women of *The Disheveled Maidens* appear in public with their hair loose, dyed blonde, wild, or curly (*despletite*). Thus although no mention of tightly-braided hair pertains to the feminine characters of *The Disheveled Maidens*, and even though through the course of events they do become spiritually disheveled or distraught, the novel's title in Romanian, *Fecioarele despletite*, translated *The Disheveled Maidens*, serves as an outright sign that Papadat-Bengescu's women, having long lost their virginity, purity, and innocence, have ceased to adhere to traditional cultural norms.[4]

The association of a woman's unbraided hair with sexual depravity appears early on in the novel when Mini speaks of a woman who had just given birth to a baby, born as if from her blond, snake-like curls:

> I saw a young girl, wearing a yellow silken shirt under her hospital gown, bending over a little yellow worm of a baby she was holding in her lap. A huge wave of curly blond hair hung spread over her face; through the golden snakes of this adornment, I could hardly make out a withered, ugly face. Surely, that poor yellowish larva had been born from that amazing hair. (42)

Beyond these provocative and modernist representations of femininity, the narrative focus is on Lenora's frequent breakdowns and general depression largely caused by her secret adulterous affair with an Italian painter that led to the birth of Mika-Lé and on Lenora's final departure from the Hallipas' Prundeni estate to Bucharest to seek treatment in Doctor Walter's Sanatorium. As the trilogy's first novel ends, under the excellent care of Doctor Walter, Lenora recovers and makes a full and public confession of Mika-Lé's illegitimate birth. Although such a confession causes Lenora's divorce, it also derails Mika-Lé's plan to extort money from the Hallipa family.

On an immediate level, the novel's characters resemble puppets moved by strings of sexual desire, and what moves the plot in each episode is sexual impulse.[5] Lenora Hallipa, for instance, who "had gained precocious knowledge of all aspects of life" (68), discovers early on the sexual power she has over men. Having had her share of sexual encounters, as well as a first husband, from a large supply of military officers stationed in her native, provincial town of Mizil, she then marries young Doru Hallipa, the sole heir of a sizeable fortune complete with a family estate. As the new mistress of the beautiful mansion, Lenora is "a haughty nymph lustily sprawl[ed] on the bed of her conjugal love" (9).

In *The Disheveled Maidens*, no less than in the other two novels, Papadat-Bengescu seems determined to show that sex should be recognized as the controlling and directing force that it is. Sexuality, firm and insistent in its pressure, is what ultimately gets communicated from the inarticulateness of Lenora, as she clings to Doru's arms and lips. Registering another dimension of Lenora's insatiable sexuality, her seduction by the Italian painter has far reaching and devastating effects. Its silent and lascivious echoes still haunting the deserted hallways of the Prundeni mansion materialize in the perfidious sexuality of Mika-Lé and ultimately cause the collapse of the Hallipa's old world.

Like the novel's women, men too appear to be activated by sexual impulses only. Doru Hallipa, Lenora's husband and sexual puppet whose "bondage was absolute" (9), is passionate about his horses and a first-class rider "who pulls hard at the reins" (13). On the heels of his divorce from Lenora, Hallipa is back in high sexual gear in his pursuit of Eliza, the fiancée he had once abandoned after being seduced by the experienced Lenora in his youth. The rapid pace of Hallipa's sexual advances offers the image of a man [Hallipa] "with the gait of a hunter tired by the chase, taking his prey to his den. Eliza, clinging on to Doru's arm, dragging her narrow shoes, look[ing] like a swamp duck in the damp air; a panting, hot sheepish game" (126).

Further substantiating its demonstrable eroticism that actively transgresses characterization, *The Disheveled Maidens* displays a deep sensitivity to the spatiality of desire. The very shapes of rooms and spaces in the Hallipa's mansion are invested with a libidinal charge. What appears to be more commanding and thrilling that the plot is the erotic power, and oblique possession in which jouissance is derived from a moment of erotic tension that is scenically conceived.[6] And even though the Italian painter who once seduced Lenora is just a dimly-perceived, long-gone figure who no longer achieves sexual possession of Lenora's body, he continues to take oblique possession of a space infused with erotically charged power that is still capable of subjecting Lenora to its own libidinal force. Ultimately, oblique possession involves an eroticism that thrives on the dissolution of the sexes, male and female, into the scene of *jouissance* that makes it not only impossible but also unnecessary to picture the lovers' individual identities clearly. What is left is a veritable spatialization of desire with such spatial elements as the painted ceiling in the Hallipas' mansion – an "absurd ceiling like a summer sky, with cotton-like balloons of white clouds against a jarring blue, [where] you could imagine them [the lovers] playing an absurd pantomime, with broken gestures" (27).

A realm comprised of erotic spaces, the Hallipas' Prundeni mansion offers the overall spatial effect of a "peaceful yet sensitive body" (13). From the architecturally erotically inscribed gate to the estate, which obliquely announces the possessive pathway Doru takes each time he enters the mansion to gain access to Lenora's voluptuously draped body, to Lenora's "white, pink and mauve alcove, full of lace and ribbons in amorous and naïve colors, with angels on the ceiling and roses on the walls" (19), there is a strongly suggested scene of eroticism. And although as a whole the Prundeni mansion manages to be a space of inordinately untempered monotony, as a conjugal domain it bears a corporeal or phallic dimension captured in the sense of things: "the grandfather clock with gentle shades" (3); "the limpid voice of the bronze tongue [of the clock] striking another quarter"; "the bronze chords in the large ebony piano" (12); and the unfinished vestibule, where Mini, who sarcastically calls it "the Shakespearean setting of the tragedy" (26), notices

> the gradual shade of the naked, smooth, round columns, left in the visible plaster stone... that Hallipa's hieratic complexion, the tortured, Medusa-like head on Lenora's goddess-like body. ... The same unpolished, sandy mosaic on the floor resembled a paved desert in which you could imagine your steps melt down noiselessly. Then the chalky white of the walls up to mid-height, and, above, the foolish paintings: the Pompeian frames and the panels with nymphs and angels, the same nymphs that poorly resembled Lenora and the same plump angels. (26-27).

This space of desire, like others in The *Disheveled Maidens*, is one in which contingent desire has not been organized metaphorically, definitionally into sexuality. Rather, the characters' imprint takes oblique possession of the spaces, a possession that does not involve physical penetration of the space, but does amount to a metaphoric penetration of the space's overall character. It is as if sex in Papadat-Bengescu's world were almost the only imaginable form of personal interchange since all other contacts have been reduced to the account other characters give of their interactions. Nevertheless, sex in *The Disheveled Maidens* does not enrich relationships beyond what they initially were. It is merely the instrument of a compulsion to have a relationship or a marriage, a compulsion aroused by a whole complex of inarticulate excitations about the representative glamor of a particular person. At the end of what in most novels would be very complicated human attachments, Papadat-Bengescu's characters simply walk off, stumbling into other sexual liaisons: in the second novel of the trilogy, *A Concert of Music by Bach*, Lenora is married to Doctor Walter and Doru Hallipa to Eliza.

This curious sequence showing that nothing has been accumulated from the tangled relationships that hold two people, points to the fact that nothing of a personal kind modifies a person in a human relationship as much as being in a relationship to an external force. Assembled from Mini's inner thoughts and commentaries, the novel's abundant city imagery provides vignettes of people meaningfully related to the scenery of urban energy. Imagining the city as a belt, Mini "felt it there, around her. A belt so close and so precious that it seemed to be made of the very fibers that sustain the diffuse substances of our own body within our structure, which by its consistence girdles the fluid dispersion of our blood" (76).

Papadat-Bengescu's choice of a feminine narrator as the woman embedded in the city is probably no coincidence. According to Aaron Betsky, "we often personify cities as women, which are seen as realms of femininity as opposed to the masculinity of nature. In fact, one of the recurrent themes in Western history, from the Song of Songs to the stories of the Moors in Spain, is that of the rulers who conquer or build a city who is then feminized by the women living in it" (32).[7]

In the city Mini is the embodiment of the middle-class woman who manages to create a powerful space for herself, a domain that reaffirms her femininity. Much of *The Disheveled Maidens* focuses on Mini, who becomes part of the spectacle of the city by roaming its indeterminate space and by continually observing and reporting the changing composition of forms, colors, and textures into which all inhabitants are dissolving.

Mini's response to Bucharest too can be illuminated in the light of oblique possession. The city, which she sees as "noble, vast, luminous … giving you a feeling of healthy, tender joy" (43), is Mini's own space of desire. Here she feels "her heart throbbing" and her lips wet with the drizzling rain "wetting them like juice" (128). Even when she finds herself at night in parts of the city that she does not know very well and that she can barely make out through the shroud of evening frost, Mini is "afraid as of something that couldn't really hurt, while the place, even if unknown, was, nevertheless, familiar, as though, with closed eyes, she'd been in well-known arms" (52).

The streets, the streetcars, everything that manages to produce this obliquely possessive sense is the very citadin space, with all the energy that its intense, both confusing and exciting, activities generate. Thanks to her traveling through the city – a zone of veritable quicksand, a magical land, free of interaction between individual persons, so fascinating and so arresting – Mini is able to associate herself contiguously with it, to take in the sense of the breathless scenes with their staccato rhythm.

A sprightly figure within the magical city, with "her heart pounding hard as if she had been handling the huge chain and the key of the sacred citadel" (55), Mini surrenders to urban experiences through a relaxation of her ego's defenses. Transposed, she unconditionally accepts and embraces the city's apparitions, "the madmen, different yet related by their exaltation…all of them decidedly showing one common trait: they were all starved, of bread, of meat, of people, of life. Hungry! Their insanity was that of hunger" (42). Filled with an all-possessing desire to rush forward and embrace her beloved city and "the immense multitude of people (55)," Mini joins with the countless throng and becomes a part of the great current of city life.

Papadat-Bengescu spares no effort in highlighting the Romanian capital in the interwar period, which was also Bucharest's golden age. Much enlarged by the peace treaties at the end of WWI, Romania, and especially Bucharest, became a Mecca for European and American travelers. Writers and journalists like Emil Hoppe, John McCulloch, Paul Morand, James T. Shotwell and John Reed, the American war correspondent who found Bucharest "sunk in luxury and sloth,"[8] spent time in the capital, as did the famous Countess Waldeck, the Times correspondent.

In her book *Athéné Palace*, published a little over a decade earlier than *The Disheveled Maidens*, Waldeck wrote extensively about Bucharest as a city "irresistibly between East and West, between ancient and modern, between rustic and metropolitan…[where] people came because it was the terminal of all traffic between Europe and the Orient, and a stop here was necessary on the way to and from more or less mysterious missions" (257).[9] Her descriptions of the city turn into picture-like images, such as the ones capturing winter in Bucharest when "a thick fur of white padded everything, lying in luscious cushions on the cupolas of the hundred-odd Byzantine churches;" or the Bucharestians who "exposed themselves to the temptations of the Calea Victoriei – the latest Paris perfumes, English woolens, Vienna leather goods, and mountains of salami, candies, and *marron glacés…* and lingered in the *Cartea Românească*, the Brentano's of Bucharest, where you could get books in every language" (258-9).

Through Mini's eyes, *The Disheveled Maidens* may appear as a chronicle of Bucharest's golden days, "an admirable epoch, … in which there were samples of all generations moving about" (77), but also of the site of a new world, where men and women mixed, where "women … could have walked about smoothly and majestically in a peplum [even] when there were so many forms of transition towards a plastic pattern of the future" (77), and where all people could construct their own identities. Substantiating Papadat-Bengescu's own view that "towns … possess a power of their own which fights and conquers all the laws of nature" (29), the characters of *The Disheveled Maidens* live in an ever-changing realm, full of possibilities, where

> the numerous Pleiades of intellectuals ravaged by the violent outburst of the war [WWI] were carved into reduction by the new diet and the new morality. They were the ones who didn't make up a nation, but represented it on all occasions where aspect was the essential requirement; those of the first rank placed in the first row at all spectacles.

> Yet ... the ones seated behind them were exactly those that comprised the reserve forces, the most important ones, the surprise and the resources of production, the commissioning of the latest moral and anatomical
> novelty. (77)

In the rapid rise to prominence of new groups of people in the city, Elena Hallipa's husband, Jorj Drăgănescu, stands for the increasingly urbanized and industrialized class of Bucharestians – not only in the scale and pace of economic development and change, but also in the values and mores of the varied socio-economic classes newly created. With money becoming the predominant measure of all value in society, Drăgănescu's family progresses from its modest beginnings as innkeepers to an ever-expanding class of *nouveau riche* – a journey marked by the trajectory from Old Mother Tar, Drăgănescu's mother who "used to tar the old stale barrels [to store the family's wine] from a tar pot" (58), to Drăgănescu's rise as vice-president of the Chamber of Commerce and venture capitalist. His marriage to Elena Hallipa, a daughter from the class of the landed gentry, and their elegant home on one of Bucharest's most fashionable streets, Lascăr Catargiu, confirm the old adage of the solidity and stability of land being progressively undermined by the culture of money.

Duplicating Drăgănescu's "*noblesse de baril*," which is what Mini calls Drăgănescu's recent social elevation, is the ambitious flour magnate, the *parvenue* Ada Razu. One of the most snobbish girls in the fashionable dancing halls, this "queen of flour" (53) marries the feeble Prince Maxențiu, the landowner from Plăieşele, who was once engaged to Elena Hallipa. The Prince, who moves to the city after selling his land, follows the same pattern as Doru Hallipa, the agent of patriarchal tradition and a "rustic feudal lord," who sells the Prudeni country estate and becomes transformed by the town and the present times "into a poor bourgeois, bringing only the cloth of a tent he might pitch on the edge of the town with him" (111). In the incredible fluidity of Bucharest's socio-economic system, both Hallipa and Prince Maxențiu stay "a component in decomposition ... scattered around the living city as separate individuals, pieces severed from a decomposed whole, for each of them to become an initial spring of new activity" (127). Addressing indirectly the acute concern about pressures on landlord culture and its fading role in the culture of the nation, the two landlords' move to the city makes clear that the city is "a haven ... the Promised Land" to which they come "to conquer life where its pulse had the richest beat" (39). Itself a space of desire, Bucharest is the fertile ground where distinct new species could be identified, where order and the virtues developed in the country continued to fall apart, and where morality was questioned – "the slum girl had disappeared or become exotic, and the new plebeian professions, typewriting and manicure, had changed the face of the slums. The taxi driver was the quintessence of the slum boy, coached through mechanics as through fire, to assume the select form which yesterday still used to lead to 'anything'" (78).

Young women like Mika-Lé, who in the morally rigid system of the country did not conform to the dictates of respectability, become in the city exemplars of the increasingly urbanized crowd that differed dramatically from the family-oriented culture that had characterized Romania to that point. Unlike another socially constructed female of the time, the prostitute, the loose woman of Mika-Lé's type, is loose only from the bounds of a moralized space, like that of the traditional world of the Hallipas where Lenora's "bizarre example of moral adultery" (26) singles out and penalizes the potentially traumatic consequences of casual sex.

Created out of a related but distinct set of social anxieties and associated therefore with a different moral geography of the city, these new women are the disheveled maidens who enjoy their freedom, their individuality, and their power to do pretty much as they like. Seeking their own fulfillment, they reveal that they are full of sexual passion and desire. As in the process of giving in to their passions, they follow the course of sexual deviance as they "shed the burdens of their sins by hurriedly giving birth to sons fathered by absinth or punch" (41).

Like the women of Western cities, the disheveled maidens of Bucharest also bore the anxieties connected with mass consumer culture, mainly because they belonged in the major class of consumers as the group whose identity was focused on outward appearance. And since Bucharest was the economic capital of Romania, it was also the first place in which mass culture and consumerism were made manifest in the landscape by what the morally upright called the "desiring" women.[10] Unforgettably portrayed in the excerpt that follows, such desiring women, or disheveled maidens, are reprepresented by a model with the professional perfection of the cover girl, a woman with very narrow hips and wearing the latest fashions. To Mini she appears as

> something between a puppet and a woman; with thick eyeliner on her eyelashes and eyelids so that her eyes looked like two black spots on their chalk-white face; her hair, short at the nape, while at the front she wore it as a curly tousle, violently peroxided and so high that it exceeded the tiny, wrinkled face.
>
> She used to walk around in ball gowns of a nakedness that induced no trace of impudence in the aspect of her absent body, and this could

> cheat customers, while in the fiery tuft of her hair she displayed the insolent glory of an immense egret. Or she would disappear in the rigid circumference of hoop-skirted flounces, in some stylish model, her forehead tightly bound with some broad ribbon, which made her head look quite morbid.
>
> She was a regular night customer of restaurants frequented by foreigners, in which drinking, not love making, was the main vice, and that she was reputed for her prim attire and her everlasting insomnia. Night after night she kept staring at the yellowish liquid in the permanently filled glasses! ... Who knows what caprice of alcohol or betrayal of sleep had once dishonored the artifice of her barren orgies. (41)

Also known as "painted" women, such demimondes who inhabited city spaces represented a particularly potent and obvious form of transgressive behavior, a specific type of (im)morality.[11] Since their attractiveness was based on the skill with which they disguised their real looks, either through make up or stylish clothes, they used fashion to hide their true selves. Related to sexual passion and fueled by it, their passion for clothes and dry goods, their idleness, their boredom and their vanity led them down the perilous path of over consumption.

The disheveled maidens of the city were everything a traditional woman was not supposed to be. This is why there is so much anxiety expressed in the novel around Lenora's or Mika-Lé's giving in to their sexual passions or around the painted woman's fascination with outward appearance and dress. Both types of indulgence not only upset the precarious balance between self-control and self-indulgence, but also lead to societal changes. Morality could not be mapped so easily in the big city where the emerging spaces of consumerism did not distinguish between ladies and painted women, respectable citizens and charlatans, those who were good and those who were evil:

> In the simultaneous game of transformations you couldn't tell whether they were born from literature or were the very models from which extreme literature was born. Baudelaire and Verlaine, two classicists when you read them now, were circulating in thousands of human forms and the decadent man was the normal everyday man, at whom their older brothers still looked in amazement, and who could hardly wait to become a classic in his turn and to be replaced .

> Under torturous appearances, simple souls were taking pains to lead complicated lives, while dubious characters lived under old and honest firms. What lunacy! (78-9)

Thus although Mini's focus tended to elide immoral behavior, she had to acknowledge from her friend Nory's reports respectable houses that hide upstairs brothels and respectable girls who are prostitutes in the living city. While informing Mini of Mika-Lé's whereabouts, for example, Nory also talks about the young girl's new quarters in Autumn Street:

> A lot of doors open into the so-called refectory of this honorable boarding house. Two long tables covered with oilcloths and vases holding paper flowers, both pushed to the wall; a ruin of a piano, a large iron stove; a merry and cheap life ...True enough, they do eat poorly, but the boys come up with supplements ...Do you know, Mini, that the boss in Autumn Street is the divorced wife of A., the master of the Bar Association? She is worn out. She is ugly and "evil," as Lina would say. She patronizes at the head of the table with her "fancy man," her pimp, at her right side. The little rooms on the entresol and the garret are for "youngsters;" they let them now on credit, now on installments. On the first story she has rooms fit for couples "just passing through" or eloping. It is the specialty of the house. They get separate room service ... In the afternoons the bosses retire to play poker arranged around thievery. (105)

In Papadat-Bengescu's *The Disheveled Maidens*, Bucharest appears as an all-consuming and magnetic capital that suggests the Western capitals, complete with its assortment of houses of ill-repute and street apparitions, like the one Mini sees often wear[ing]

> a long riding coat with nothing underneath in the middle of winter and a pot hat; he had a black beard and held an old leather briefcase in his hand; he had a serious, wise air, was walking calmly, with equal steps, chasing women along the same way, between Alcalay and Socec, uttering a sort of prayer, which, at its end, begged in ecclesiastical terms, "charity for love." A hungry beggar that gave you a strange fear by this participation of God in the insanity of the world. (42)

Having traversed the space of almost six centuries from its first mentioned as a mere residence on the Danubian plain recorded in 1459 by the Wallachian ruler Vlad Țepeș,[12] the Romanian capital is complete with the gravity of smooth, tall, imposing edifices that lined up perfectly and with its inhabitants coming from all parts of the country:

> The passers-by were numerous, and they were trying to squeeze between those people on the Central Canal of the city, that stretch of confluence between the Palace and the boulevard. They stopped for a moment at the corner of the Elisée to prepare for their crossing. The National Theatre was standing there in its tiny square; old, but still preserving some grandeur. Like two affluent streams, one illuminated, the other obscure, Câmpineanu and Matei Millo Street flowed down by its sides, providing a little waving on the plain of Bucur's grazing field. (57)

As Mini looks in the translucent fog toward the novel's end, she embraces the city she loves. Earlier on, in the rain, she had "compared her soul to that of Master Manole's wife" who, immured alive in the walls of the church built by her husband, becomes one with his creation.[13] Like Ana, the Master's wife who hurries through the flood and the rain to reach the church with the food she is taking to her husband, Mini projects herself in an emerging metaphor of identification with the city, her master toward whom she is forever rushing "with her brave little feet ... hurrying ahead relentlessly ... soaked in the streams ... undefeated in the yearning to arrive carrying in her little hands the food of the master, protected and kept warm by the heat of her palms" (113).

Mini's love of and focus on Bucharest, the living city, is a potent indication of the importance of the capital in the critical decades of the 1920s and 1930s both in terms of economic growth of the city and of the expansion of its built form. To the architect-designed ornate office and government structures, the city experienced the construction of two types of public places: those that served to display its cultural status (e.g., theaters, museums, parks) and those that served consumer demands (e.g., stores, restaurants, dance halls). Mentioned in Mini's description of the city, the National Theatre and the Museum of Art, as well as the Capşa and the Nestor restaurants and coffee shops, were landmarks inscribed into Bucharest. Like New York or Chicago in *Sister Carrie*, Bucharest becomes for modern Romania "part of the hieroglyph of the race"[14] – the space of a network of public spaces within the city that were characterized by the activities of consumption and the display of social status. Of particular interest is that a good deal of these spaces were open to, in fact catered to, women – women defined first and foremost by the fact that they were Bucharestians flourishing in the city's public spaces.

Among these women Mini is a powerful presence. Encoded in the cityscape, she offers an alternative cultural panorama of modern Romania, one that does not shut out the old order but reframes it as a set of vignettes – large owners like Doru Hallipa or Prince Maxenţiu who were unable or unwilling to maintain their manorial estates; the domestic code of country life dissipated from within to make room for unions like that of Elena Hallipa (the old gentry) and Drăgănescu (capitalist entrepreneur); or the rise of urban life, energized by its disregard of a stable, ordained order and by the release of a destructive extemporizing energy, such as Mika-Lé's.

Carefully controlled through Mini's diffused perspective, *The Disheveled Maidens* presents a new society that subtly reformulates gender roles. It offers a different model of manliness – domestically submissive to women, sexually controlled and socially inept – and inscribes a new sphere for women. Both elevated and contained as fashionable figures or endlessly false appearances, Lenora the "haughty nymph," Nory the feminist, Cousin Lina the doctor, the snobbish Elena Hallipa Drăgănescu, and the sexually *outrée* Mika-Lé are just a few of the disheveled maidens, the new types of femininity that help articulate Papadat-Bengescu's view of the nation's modern, feminine identity.

And the moment was certainly ripe for Papadat-Bengescu's views. In a city filled with theater-going crowds, Ibsen's plays were among the most staged productions of Romanian theater's repertoires. Plays like *Ghosts* and *A Doll's House* were extremely popular in the 1920s, a time when Romanian society was engaged in and witnessed the dialectical struggle between the country's old and new epochs. As bourgeois tragedies, both *Ghosts* and *A Doll's House* conformed to Friedrich Hebbel's manifesto on the genre expounded in his preface to *Maria Magdalena* (1844). Reflecting on great drama that occurs only in periods of historical change, Hebbel points out that modern tragedy will show how the warring elements of the new age "are begetting a new form of humanity…in which woman will once again stand face to face with man, as man stands face to face with society."[15] Taking his notes from Hebbel, Ibsen crafts in his two plays a dramatic tension whose power springs from its female protagonists' poisonous submission to the ideal of "woman place."[16]

Seizing on the contemporary feminist debate, the Hallipa trilogy's second novel, *A Concert of Music by Bach*, brings into the Romanian literary landscape of the period more attention to the status of women and to previously disregarded dimensions of women's psychology. Replete with most of the same characters in *The Disheveled Maidens*, *A Concert of Music by Bach* is also a feminocentric novel that serves as a basis for a "developing female aesthetic"[17] and deals with an admission within socially prescribed limitations of a new, assertive femininity ranging from emotionalism to conscientious choices of reproductivity, domestic arrangements and nurturing capacity. Unlike their subservient predecessors in male writers' fiction, Papadat-Bengescu's female characters show the warring elements of the new age. Their susceptibility to music and romance and their concern with their professional and social status challenge the relegation of women to a position inferior to that of men as incompatible with modern life, and, therefore, contribute to changing the conventional notions of what constitutes femininity and women's place in Romanian society and culture.[18]

In their leading roles, the feminine characters of *A Concert of Music by Bach* shape their own self-image and generate a conscious portrayal of femininity that inscribes, but is not limited to, the needs and pleasures of women's bodies, the assertion of their powerful emotions (especially romantic and erotic love) and the nuanced range of their transformative sensibility. Unlike the old "ruined" or "less-than-perfect" women victimized by romantic obsessions, the women of A *Concert of Music by Bach* face desires and choices that shape – rather than detract from – their worth and destinies. Luscious voluptuousness, affairs, illegitimate births, and so forth end up as sites that question patriarchy's continuing obsessions with female sexual purity, or sinful womanhood, to proclaim the legitimacy of the heroines as serious subjects defying the social and sexual constraints placed upon women by class and gender.

Relying on the literary topos of feminine emotions to challenge the dominant hegemony of early-twentieth-century Romanian society's culturally constructed sensibility, *A Concert of Music by Bach* spatializes the relations between the novel's women protagonists and the social order, while simultaneously constructing and defining feminine emotions and a woman's social, sexual, and psychological identity. Confronting the ambiguities of women's position in society, and not just the clear-cut models of woman's social degradation or ascendancy, the novel uses three central characters to institute a dialogue between reality and fiction: Elena Drăgănescu, whose wretched marriage serves to fulfill her misplaced sense of honor within bourgeois norms of morality; Doctor Lina Rim, who sacrifices the most elementary human emotions to marry so as to fulfill societal norms; and the *parvenue*-turned-wealthy socialite, Ada Razu, who finds desire outside the institution of marriage. In the triology's second novel, these protagonists' skillfully interwoven stories provide the narrative circumstances that frame a woman's inner psychic space while simultaneously questioning and asserting her social role and identity.

By identifying the ways in which social hegemony works on feminine emotions, Papadat-Bengescu seems to suggest ways in which feminine emotions also work on patriarchal hegemony, how certain feminine emotions deemed as "inappropriate" socially, such as desiring a man other than one's husband or failing to nurture one's own child, need to be subject to reinterpretation and revision as ideas are generally.

Realizing, like other prominent writers of her time, such as Kate Chopin or Charlotte Perkins Gilman, that the cult of the domestic interior fixes the modern definition of femininity, Papadat-Bengescu emphasizes in her writing the possibilities of the interior as a place of self-definition within the parameters of the rapid and aggressively growing culture of early-twentieth-century Romania. Encapsulating the bare bones of an increasingly bourgeois life, the sumptuous domestic interiors of the Drăgănescu s' mansion featured in *A Concert of Music by Bach* create a new stage for Elena Drăgănescu, a place that is not only imprisoning but also potentially empowering as a space of charged emotions and of setting for most of the narrative. As a place charged with empowering conclusions about gender and gender relations, it ultimately displaces the isolated and the local to allow for the construction of a wider unity with other similar spaces expanding into the collective tapestry of feminine emotion, what Adrienne Rich describes as "your own house as a tiny fleck on an everwidening landscape, the center of it all from which the circles expanded into the infinite."[19]

In a meandering and ingeniously conceived narrative that details, catalogs, and individualizes women's emotions within a public system regulated by psychological and moral norms, *A Concert of Music by Bach* focuses on the three couples generated by the three principal feminine characters: the doctors Rim whose loveless marriage pairs Lina, a women's doctor, with her hypochondriac academic/psychologist husband; the dying Prince Maxențiu and his wife Ada, who is engaged in a game of seduction with a local *bon vivant* and avid horseman, Lică the Troubadour; and the wealthy, *nouveau riche* Drăgănescu and his beautiful wife, Elena, Lenora Hallipa's daughter, whose emerging love for the musician Marcian defies the artificiality of her marriage.

The novel opens with a detailed description of the Rims' house and the introduction of Lina Rim, who stands for the female representation of patriarchy's obsession with female sexual purity. While fighting all her life to defend herself from being labeled a "fallen woman", she relies on her work as a women's doctor and on a pathetic marriage to negotiate her "respectable" place in society. Although she provides almost full financial support of her unkind and demanding husband Rim, she lives within a patriarchy as a gendered subaltern.[20] Unwilling to challenge conventional morals, she conforms to a monstrously narrow notion of women's honor, grounded on the basic misogynist principle that woman is sexually evil and must therefore be controlled and confined by marriage, an institution that Lina feels will purify her. Living with contradictions, she positions herself as a submissive nurse to an aloof and disappointing husband, who stays home most of the time, except for the rare occasions when he teaches university courses that consist mainly of a series of veiled sexual advances directed at his female students. A violin and flute player, Rim never misses a chance to make fun of Lina's lack of refinement and aesthetic taste, without ever taking into account her credentials as a reputable doctor at a time when the profession was just beginning to include women.

As the improbable mother to Sia, Lina's unscrupulously defeminized and plain daughter conceived during a brief romance in her early youth with her cousin, Lică the Troubadour, Lina has kept her motherhood a secret to all, including her husband Rim, and has played no part in Sia's upbringing.

Labeled "kind-hearted" throughout the narrative as a matter of ironic reflection, with her thickset, grotesque, and strident body, Lina is an *arriveste* professional with a lower-class background who strived to acquire a house that cost "everything I [Lina] earned in a lifetime, plus an inheritance of Rim and a lot of debts" and where "the battery of aluminum pans and pots [vie with] her forceps" (137). Furnished with mediocre objects – the marble stairs, the new porcelain stove, and tall doors painted in pink with loud golden stripes – Lina's house possesses both a laboratory-like shining brightness and the complementary appearance of a luxurious mausoleum. Her decision to throw her daughter Sia out of her house after a brief stay, and Sia's subsequent death from an untreated infection resulting from a botched abortion complicated by an ectopic pregnancy (a double damnation given Lina's profession), deny Lina her professional reputation as a bedrock of goodness and compassion and expose the horrors of her home and of her image as an ostensibly "good" woman. On an emotional level, she can only deceive and destroy; in her case, the necessity of gender as fate is weighed down on the scale of conduct by the fact that Lina is given a choice.

The underlying principle of Lina's character is precisely the same as in Ibsen's *Ghosts*, namely, "the immortality of conventional morals."[21] Having submitted to her husband as a good and subservient wife, Lina hides her daughter's identity to protect her wretched marriage. But when Rim becomes sexually involved with Sia, the years of married wretchedness begin to expose the hypocrisy of social conventions. Furthermore, Lina's effort to bury herself in the confinement of respectable wifehood is deadly and pernicious, not only to herself but also to Sia. As emotionally inexpressive as the girl might be, she communicates the negative affective energy that inhabits the social space between mother and daughter. Having conformed to society's ideal of proper behavior, Lina is responsible for enormous destructiveness and is responsible for Sia's tragic life and death.

Like Helene Alving, the heroine of *Ghosts*, Lina Rim dooms herself and her child by her own acts. For Papadat-Bengescu, as for Ibsen, male control of female sexuality is one of history's tyrannical ghosts that make both heroines agents and victims burdened by their cowardice; but in making Lina Rim a doctor, Papadat-Bengescu accords to this female protagonist the tragic failure of making a choice, one that imprisons her and kills her daughter. Lina's refusal to acknowledge her child and her lifelong fear of being exposed as an unwed mother dramatize patriarchy's most important mechanism for maintaining woman in her powerless place: male control of female sexuality.

If the Rim's story questions the patriarchal order and its established morality, the marriage of Prince and Princess Ada Maxenţiu points to the fluidity of a society in transition, its social mores and manners and opportunities tied to sexual seduction.

Spontaneous and full of life, Ada Maxenţiu embodies the defiance of free spirit, sexual desire and natural instinct over the social rules governing her social milieu. Humiliated in her youth as the flour queen, a nickname indicative of both her low birth and the plebian source of her immense wealth, Ada has married Prince Maxenţiu for the title and aristocratic position that such a union would bring. Next to the tuberculosis-wrecked Prince, "pale as wax and with red eyes and stained eyelids" (162), she is a wild figure that resists assimilation and endangers her husband's frail masculinity. A threatening other who spells trouble to the social and patriarchal order, she is an affirmation of free will, independence and liberation to those who would look at her through the lenses of feminist theory; at the same time, to those informed by post-colonial theory, Ada unmasks the Romanian culture's misogynist and racial undertones toward the other.

To Lică the Troubadour who first sees her when she rides with the Prince in the dog cart that nearly runs him over, Ada appears as "a Gypsy woman as desiccated as a devil, her lips as red as coagulated blood and a pair of burning eyes beneath the leather cap that adorned her, sharpening her already sharp chin even more" (162). Although he is a good-for-nothing whose life largely gravitates around his affairs with "wenches," Lică possesses a social pedigree. By being the brother of beautiful Lenora Hallipa, currently married to the respected Doctor Walter, Lică is also the uncle of the elegant and wealthy Elena Drăgănescu, married to one of Bucharest's wealthiest men. Thus, in the hegemonic geometry of center and periphery of Romania's patriarchal system that conditions all perceptions of self and the other, Lică is in a hegemonic male-subject position. Ada is his inferior, because as a woman she is a subaltern gender and as a Gypsy she is the non-white and non-Romanian marginalized other who reinforces Lică's cultural hegemony.

After being hired as Prince Maxenţiu's horse trainer through Ada's intercession, Lică maintains his defiant air toward her. In a memorable scene in the stables, ready to quit because he can no longer stand the domineering attitude and screaming of "the Gypsy bitch," Lică hits her hard across the hands with a horsewhip. Following on the heels of this scene is a violent seduction, which Lică initiates and which Ada invites. But even after the two become lovers, Lică continues to feel the same mixture of attraction and aversion toward Ada, an ambivalence which reveals his deep-seated anxieties about gender, race, class, nation, and sexuality.

In the novel's complex socio-cultural conceptualization, Papadat-Bengescu's portrayal of Ada epitomizes the ambiguity of the Romanian male consciousness, its perception of Gypsy women as the highly marked and racialized other, associated with assorted displays of a rebellious, subversive, and free spirit. This ambiguity reveals the need to tame, to control, and to neutralize ultimately the demonic Gypsy woman. In a triumph of gender power relations, the Prince's death frees Ada, whose title and wealth are now available to Lică as the ultimate spoils of his sexual conquest.

If there is any evidence in the physical actions and interactions of Papadat-Bengescu's characters that gender and feminine sensibility are either metaphorically or actually enacted in the performative medium of Bach's music, it rests within the narrative possibilities of the third marriage. Here Papadat-Bengescu uses music as a narrative background to link explicitly instrumental music with the social world. More specifically, Bach's music – representative of an instrumental music tradition that was able to cast off the verbal reference largely because its composers and audiences had inherited an extensive vocabulary for the articulation of affect and topos – serves as a site where skilled musicians engender affective communication without words and listeners learn to grasp the significance of given melodic shapes, rhythms, and instruments. (This vocabulary is still alive, albeit somewhat modified over time, in the music of film and advertisements, as it made possible over time the symphony's "emancipation of language.")

The prosperous industrialist Drăgănescu and his wife Elena are, in the novel's narrative present, the capital's most celebrated andenticing couple. While her marriage to Drăgănescu, which has produced a son, serves to illustrate and reproduce the patriarchal structure of power, Elena has opened her elegant home to musical *soirées* that have evolved into the capital's most talked-about cultural events. Lost in a material world and luxurious home where the border between her body, her clothes, her jewelry, and her furniture has become increasingly hard to find, Elena appears at first to be in harmony with her life that focuses on her love for music and on organizing musical events. As the rehearsals occasioned by the artistMarcian's preparation of a concert of music by Bach unravels Elena's most powerful feminine impulses, the transformative power of music conjures up the socially prescribed limitations and spiritually impoverished marriage of the Drăgănescus.

Bach's biographer and fellow organist Albert Schweitzer discovered in the composer's music something he called "the lexicon of Bach's musical speech."[22] What Schweitzer was seeing embedded in the scores, more than hearing in the music, was Bach's deployment of the musical rhetorical figures to carry the affection of the musical message. Widespread at the time, the doctrine of affections, by which musical figures had been demonstrated empirically to evoke specific emotional reactions, reported that Baroque audiences were prone to swoon, wail, weep, and shout for joy at just the right moments. "It cannot be otherwise that an individual's temperament is moved and controlled through well-written music," according to Andreas Werckmeister, "for an individual is both inwardly and outwardly, spiritually and physically, a divinely created harmonic being."[23]

Bach's music was a symbol of a bygone world set at the tipping point between the ancient and the modern, a music that takes in the tumult of the eighteenth century: the legacy of the Reformation, wars and conquests, and the birth of the Enlightenment. Most importantly, Bach's music tells the story of that confrontational moment when the "outdated" world of the Enlightment came face to face with the cold certainty of Reason. If Papadat-Bengescu's title is to be read connotatively, the sound of the music in the novel is a metaphor for registering the meeting of a patriarchal culture with a feminine sensibility as implacable in its rise as the historic moment marking the birth of Reason. Therefore, if for the characters of *A Concert of Music by Bach* the sound of music in the novel bears a textlike quality registering their evolving emotions, then for the readers, immersed in the novel in the ways Bach's music is to be understood, the novel becomes a medium that potentially enables them to rethink, and to think through, the social and political place of women and feminine emotions in modern times. Like a Bach concerto whose emotional quality engages the audience's artistic sensibility beyond the familiar tone, tempo, and rhythms toward a lexicon embedded in the score, *A Concert of Music by Bach* offers its readers a compelling narrative attuned to the coded language for private, subjective feminine sensibility couched within the socially entrenched rhythms of a patriarchal culture's beliefs and worldview.

To ground my argument and further articulate music's fixed and textlike qualities, I will rely on the theoretical license stipulated in historian Joan Scott's essay "Gender: A Useful Category of Historical Analysis"[24] and philosopher Judith Butler's book *Gender Trouble: Feminism and the Subversion of Identity.*[25] Scott's view – that metaphors for gender are practically everywhere in our public and private discourse, and that tracking them tells us interesting things about ourselves and about how gender intersects with apparently ungendered parts of life – substantiates the notion that gender metaphors actually do circulate throughout a society's discourse and, even more, that gender metaphors are circulating in a society's music, in the sounds the composers choose, and, as I propose to show in the case of Papadat-Bengescu's novel, in the ways a writer constructs the narrative associations between music and the configuration of the characters' emotions and identities.

An equally important formulation for my purpose is Butler's astonishing proposition that gender is all an act. That is, both what feminists have taken to calling sex (the biological configuration of bodies) and what we call gender (the power relations expected of these bodies) result from acts that constitute identities. And since for Butler there is no originary core self that expresses identity by recognizable acts, the gendered self is the cumulative result of performances. But if gender is constituted by body performances, and if metaphors of gender are circulated through discourse, might not elements of all bodily performances be read as metaphors of gender? And if bodily performances can be constitutive of gender and metaphors for gender, then music (the performative art par excellence) may simply be regarded as a set of scripts for spelling out metaphors of gender for the performer and for those who witness the performer's art. Here then is an intellectual ground from which the Drăgănescus' marriage is a scripted text that, like Bach's music, explores the masculine and feminine played in relation to each other and in their social roles in the Romanian society of the 1920s.

To make the point of progressive portrayal and social development, it is important to note that the events chronicled in *The Disheveled Maidens* show Elena's early youth as a time when her feminine emotions were denied and ordered into the periphery. The heroine's stern face, her dark hair severely pulled back, her strong physique, and her resemblance to her paternal grandmother, all point to (1) her subservience to the patriarchal tradition in which she had been raised and (2) her marrying the wealthy and much older Drăgănescu for strictly functional reasons. Having pushed herself into the marriage the spiritless Drăgănescu after the abrupt end of her engagement to Prince Maxențiu, an episode recounted in *The Disheveled Maidens*, Elena had dutifully tried to keep a steady course during turbulent times. The sudden collapse of her parents' seemingly story-book marriage and their subsequently rushed entrances into erotic liaisons, and the socially embarrassing revelation that her sister Mika-Lé was the product of their mother's adulterous affair with a transient artist combine to form an ending series of crises at the time of Elena's coming of age.

Portrayed in the early chapters of *A Concert of Music by Bach* in her new role as a married woman, the socially ambitious Elena devotes herself to the intertwined pleasures of playing the piano in her parlor and of arranging and hosting her musical Thursdays held in the library of her home equipped with a violin, a high-quality violoncello, a harp, a flute and sufficient other complementary instruments to equip an orchestra.

The rehearsals also mark the time when Elena begins unconsciously to deconstruct her day-to-day living and allows her intense emotions to be reinscribed and rearranged within herself, in her home, and in her interactions. Bringing to light Elena's long-silenced and submerged femininity, what Betty Fridan has unforgettably termed as "the problem that has no name,"[26] the musical soirées in the Drăgănescus' home build up the evaluational change necessary to establish Elena's friendship and emotional equality with Marcian before their love can be fleshed out.

In the novel's musical dimension, Victor Marcian's role as a conductor is as much metaphorical as it is real: it is metaphorical because the role of the conductor is implicitly gendered as masculine. The conductor is masculine, not because so many individuals who live in the category are biologically male, but because the conductor identifies with the composer, and because, like the composer, he is understood to be the mind that creates patterns from sounds to which the performers' minds assign meaning. Leaving aside this consideration, Marcian's function as a composer is consolidated in the narrative. During the concert rehearsals, his is obsessed by a new rhythm and feverishly composes a pastoral from the sounds he has registered while visiting Elena's childhood home in Prundeni.

The act of making music, for the composer as for the conductor, is not limited to turning the score into sound: the musical experience includes the composer's/conductor's mobilizing of previously studied skills to make real for the audience the art of listening attentively to music and thus share the tenancy of the composer's/conductor's subject position with the co-composing ideal listener in the outpour of emotion.

Thus, when the music by Bach is played in the Drăgănescu s' home, with Marcian as conductor/composer/performer embodying the masculine, Elena is a part of the performative act as the silenced feminine. As Marcian's music draws her into a psychic intimacy, Elena is the first to open a page of score of accompaniment in moments of heightened emotional intensity when she is alone with Marcian. Marcian's invitation to have her continue her piano playing and eventually to join him in making music together has a double meaning resulting from the infusion of the feminine into the traditionally hegemonic and male-privileged mode of musical interpretation. First, by taking into account the hypothesis that in our time musical performance is always gendered feminine because it involves the body,[27] the invitation establishes Elena's femininity and invites the enactment of intimacy, for play musically and emotionally, within the power of duality implied by gender systems. Second, the invitation suggests that, just as good music requires a composer/conductor/performer and co-composer listener, an emotionally balanced relationship requires a new structure of feeling, one that is fulfilled by equalizing the masculine and the feminine.

Unlike the Rims' marriage, which is surrounded by the disharmony and cacophony suggested in the union between the violin and the flute-playing Rim and tone-deaf Lina, or the gender-charged sexuality of Lică and Ada, which transforms the engaging musical *soirées* into a conduit for Lică's official entrance into Bucharest's *grand monde*, Elena and Marcian's love is born from the enormously symbolic and sensual power generated by Bach's music.

The moment when Elena falls in love is marked by an emotional outburst – a "lost-self control," an "unaware[ness] of what she wanted" – to which Marcian, seated at the piano, reciprocates with the psychic exaltation of "a sort of delightful warm wave overwhelming him" (139).

Consummated in the affective space of the music room, Elena's and Marcian's falling in love recovers and magnifies her feminine and his artistic identity and ultimately articulates the lovers' empowerment. As the romance takes center stage, their love appears as an affirming affair for Elena, charting her passage from lifeless conjugal commitment to the assertion of the power of feminine emotions. It is a journey that transcends the masculine and the feminine dichotomy, a journey as harmonious and as beautiful as Bach's music itself.

But no matter how fulfilling, Elena's love affair leaves out much of the discussion of woman's body Papadat-Bengescu had invoked in *The Disheveled Maidens* as a location of being and site of political contention. What began in that first novel of the trilogy as a cultural progression from patriarchal repression to the liberation of the body becomes an important opportunity for further objectification of the body articulated in *The Hidden Way* the last novel of the trilogy. Significantly, the attempts in *The Disheveled Maidens* to make a style out of body parts that are not so much representational as they are built into the discourse of representation, such as Lenora's "bulk of passive flesh" (67), "her neck, where the veins stood tense under the fat white flesh" (5), her "white, muscular arms waving around in the air" (9), or her "complexion as of a blonde puppet, a Nuremberg puppet with a small red mouth and pink porcelain-like cheeks … and the large blue eyes … of limpid glass" (4), lead to placing the experiences of woman's body in the narrative center of *The Hidden Way*. Substantiating even further this conceptualization of body parts and even hair, Lenora's dyed-blonde hair, for instance, that functions in *The Disheveled Maidens* as a decorative cultural signifier, adapted to embody both the character's social function and her upper-class status in the form of an outward projection of the Prundeni's mistresses' successful rise from her humble beginnings in the small town of Mizil to the social ideal of feminine beauty in 1920s Romania, *The Hidden Way* forwards an intensified obsession with the corporeal that signals the body as symbolic of the characters' identity and as a register of gender and class anxiety.

Wondering about a suitable title to the last novel of the trilogy, Papadat-Bengescu muses in her diary over *Drumuri care nu se văd* (Roads that cannot be seen) as a preliminary choice that reveals unseen social currents and the centrality of the characters' bodies and modalities of embodiment as pivotal mechanisms at work in the text.[28] Although slightly different from such musings, the published novel's chosen title, *The Hidden Way* (1932)[29] points in similar fashion to the embeddedness of the characters' bodies as a topic implicit in the narrative representation and in the organizing psychic and social spaces that shape and map out the novel's central characters and their actions: Lenora Hallipa and her third husband, Doctor Walter, Director of the exclusive Walter Sanatorium; Coca-Aimée and Elena, Lenora's daughters from her second marriage to Doru Hallipa; and Elena's husband, the financier Ghiță (Jorj) Drăgănescu, and her lover, the virtuoso performer Victor Marcian.

Although Romanian critics have discussed *The Hidden Way* both as part of the Hallipa trilogy and as a separate work, they have not explicitly examined Papadat-Bengescu's efforts to address embodiment or the revalorization of the body as material text and texture of the novel.[30] The novel's thematic approach, which is the concept of the body[31] framed by notions of embodiment and of its cultural becoming and social engagement, finds its textual assertion in Doctor Walter's attitude and reflections. While "relaxing his mind the way one relaxes one's body in order to perceive its elasticity and restore its fitness," Doctor Walter ruminates: "I was able to do both evil and good and I will move on along a way similar to the paths that climb up slopes, wind around bends, and cross abysses, in order to chisel a tunnel into the darkness of some rock" (494).

To a greater extent than *The Disheveled Maidens*, *The Hidden* Way continues and amplifies Papadat-Bengescu's understanding of the body as scriptorial entity and enigmatic evidence, whose clues provide a paradigm for literary discourse that is at once embedded in and bears extensively the imprint of modern Romanian society and culture[32] – a view that follows Nietzsche's violent injunctions to reclaim the body as the nodal point for exploring notions of culture and the elaboration of character subjectivity. Also important to a discussion of the recovery of the body as backdrop and apparatus for the projection of the characters' subjectivity and inner truths in *The Hidden Way* is the philosophy of Maurice Merleau-Ponty. Following Nietzsche's dictates, Merleau-Ponty points out in *The Phenomenology of Perception* that the disclosure of the world necessarily entails embodiment, a condition in which "the essence of subjectivity is bound up with that of the body and that of the world."[33] The invitation to think the embeddedness of the body in the world as an intersubjective exchange simply translates as (1) a decentering of the characters' subjectivity in the very process of "fleshing" it out; and (2) a way to think about the body in the world as a dialogue between the "flesh of the body" and the "flesh of the world."[34]

Although some scenes of the novel are set in Switzerland, the world of *The Hidden Way* is primarily Doctor Walter's Barodin palace. Filled with antiques and works of art displayed in its museum, and well-known to Bucharest's elite as a place guaranteed to ameliorate the ravages of the ubiquitous metropolitan afflictions, hysteria and neurasthenia, the Barodin Palace is also the residence of the doctor, his wife, Lenora, and her daughter Coca-Aimée. Featured in the novel as a counterpart to the Barodin Palace, Elena Drăgănescu's house on the elegant Boulevard Lascăr Catargiu is not only a sumptuous residence but also a coveted meeting place of Bucharest's *beau monde*. Finally, the Bucharest of *The Hidden Way* is a significant setting in the engagement of Coca-Aimée as a young subject poised on the threshold between childhood and adulthood and as a generational and social vector that Papadat-Bengescu uses to examine the modern capital's underground culture. Fully immersed in the narrative discourse, the representation of Coca-Aimée's body is embedded in the fabric of her society and culture. As a plural entity emerging from the brutality and hostility inherent in its violation to its social reembodiment in terms of a dynamics of power in her relationship with and projected marriage to Doctor Walter, Coca-Aimée's body stages the unfolding scenario used as the novel's narrative backdrop. Similarly reflecting the power of embodiment by which the woman's body constitutes a site of social inscription, the descriptions of Lenora Hallipa's anatomical body during her suffer ring from and fight with uterine cancer carry symbolic, social, and cultural connotations communicating that the disturbance or troubling of the body is that which matters to a generation of Betlerian gender theorists.

In the new environment of the Walter Sanatorium, Lenora's emerging maternal function – defined in direct contrast to the collapse of paternal law in which, as in Dostoevsky's *The Possessed*, "fathers are repudiated, or bogus or dead" – prompts her to feel increasingly attracted to and dependent upon her own love for the narcissistic image of her own and Doru Hallipa's second daughter, Coca-Aimée, the most beautiful of Lenora's five children.[35] Without realizing that the psychic and moral cost of foreclosing a relationship with a father and paternal functions may be quite grim for her adolescent daughter, Lenora looks for comfort in Coca-Aimée's growth, accomplishments and future, to the point where she subordinates herself to an ideal of her daughter's social success that would exceed Lenora's own bounds. Since Doctor Walter's reputation as a specialist in psychological disorders and owner of the luxurious sanatorium guarantees Coca-Aimée's acceptance into the high society of Bucharest, Lenora becomes anxious to fulfill her own hopes and social ambitions for her daughter.

Coca-Aimée's sordid sexual encounter with a young rake consummated concurrently with Lenora's untimely death culminates in the physical convulsions and illness caused by her loss of virginity. The experience leaves her looking for an anchor, a point of cohesion to hold her sheltered from rupture and dissolution. Accustomed to luxury, and confident in the pact she concluded with Doctor Walter when Lenora's terminal cancer was diagnosed, Coca-Aimée is determined to marry Doctor Walter. In her mind, "her dear and admirable mother had chosen this place [the Walter Palace] for her! A good place, and one that would be occupied by the right person. No scruple troubled her; Lenora's affair with Walter had been a good contact, to which she was the natural heiress" (490).

A suggestive context for the writing of the human body not only in terms of its organic correspondence for each of the characters but also in that it works to allow each episode and setting to condition and create its own technique, Doctor Walter's Sanatorium stands in an unusually transparent relation to the narrative. Adding an emotional and spiritual enhancement to Dr. Walter's own psychic and physical healing, the elegant interior of his sanatorium emerges as a shrine, a space that establishes a new metaphor and soothing anesthetizer of both the doctor's and his patients' overwrought psyches and nerves.

As surrogate images for the Doctor's unconscious impulses, the Palace's finely crafted objects are potent icons of the Doctor's inner world that offer a silent exploration of their collector's self-conscious psychology. Traumatized in his youth by his physical experience in which the twenty-eight year old doctor acted as the sex slave of a rich patient, the fifty-year old, two-hundred-pound Salema, wife of the affluent banker Ephraim, Doctor Walter relates to the art objects around him and forges them as substitutes for his own self and as a means of making contact with the outside world. In the reprehensible climate of his sexual encounters with Salema, the possessions he acquired become sacred vessels that offer a stability and reassurance of social identity that transcended the Doctor's shame and humble beginnings. These antiques, purchased by Salema as tangible effects of trauma, allow Doctor Walter to "treat his own emotional state with sophisticated efforts of purification" (300)[36] by dispersing himself into such surrounding objects.

While reflecting Doctor Walter's latent or unconscious hostility to Salema, the sanatorium subtly emanates his desire to free himself of the anxiety that accompanies her memory. To stage the disappearance of Salema, rather than engage in the ideological mystification of his seduction, Doctor Walter reinforces her presence by having her portrait hung in a prominent place where this outward form of repetitious and redundant reminder of Salema's presence quickly assumes the guise and charge of the uncanny. The presence of the portrait results, on Doctor Walter's part, in a kind of hysterical avoidance of the inevitable question that might be ahead of him. Thus Doctor Walter's constant return to the staging of the loss of Salema provokes the implying necessity – namely, that her disappearance protects Dr. Walter's narcissistic shell. Her extraction from the Barodin Palace, ironically achieved by means of a permanent presence, leaves behind an apparent loss that frames reality and simultaneously precipitates Dr. Walter's becoming the sole owner of the Barodin Palace that Salema has bequeathed him. When Coca-Aimée first stops in front of the portrait, she calls Salema "The Donor" thus conferring a reputable identity on both the self-indulgent Salema and Doctor Walter.

Coupled with his reverence for antiques and beautiful objects that became a strategy of moral and psychological survival after Salema's death, Doctor Walter's conventional marriage to Leonora is a union which "supported his professional interests" (354) by conferring bourgeois respectability on his dubious reputation. Having engaged in a marriage that never brought Lenora to his bed, Doctor Walter feels as appreciative toward the dying Lenora as he had once felt toward his mistress and benefactor Salema, who "hadn't died, she had only disappeared; he'd been grateful to her. By dying, Lenora was now bestowing a new social status on him, the same way she had done it when he had married her, and his gratitude for her was thus growing" (460).

Furthermore, since in the marriage to Lenora Doctor Walter "wasn't separating at all Aimée from Lenora in his judgments, and in this way his marriage formed a satisfactory entity (354), "after Lenora's death he can appropriate Coca-Aimée in the art museum of the Barodin Palace in spite of his contempt for her shallowness. With her blue eyes, "white, diaphanous porcelain-like face, and golden curls" (320), Coca-Aimée gives Doctor Walter "the impression that he [is] seated before a doll" (320), an object of art that "had to be added to his collection" (499).

Paralleling and intersecting the narrative of Doctor Walter, Lenora, and Coca-Aimée, is the continuing love story of Elena Drăgănescu (Lenora's oldest daughter) and Marcian. Since, according to Coca-Aimée's shallow comment, Drăgănescu is "a rank-and-file man, an upstart with no qualities" (320), while Marcian "[is] a celebrity," Elena feels perfectly justified in her attraction to the musician. Their courtship, which was one of the central themes of *A Concert of Music by Bach*, materializes in *The Hidden Way* when they become lovers. When her husband dies in the Walter Sanatorium after a heart attack, Elena unexpectedly becomes a widow, free to be with Marcian.

The positioning of the three character triangles in *The Hidden Way* – Lenora, Coca-Aimée, and Doctor Walter; Drăgănescu, Marcian and Elena; and the intriguing feminine triptych of Coca-Aimée and her two female friends, the submissive Hilda Gert and the cold and calculated Cora Perşu – open up new conceptual possibilities for representing and understanding the performance of identity, and specifically gender identity in relation to the body and to an engagement with Romanian culture and society. At the heart of Papadat-Bengescu's text is a representation of femininity and masculinity that both enhances and moves away from the conventional gendered discourse predicated on sexuality and sexual desire of Romanian fiction. Centering on the vulnerability of identity and a physicality that does not always imply an entirely unmediated experience of the body, *The Hidden Way* reveals a series of ever-changing character representations in which the self stages its own fictionality. In this the self, even whilst acknowledging that it subscribes to a set of roles, broadcasts a message of the vulnerability of gender and class designations recalling Judith Butler's idea that subjectivity is only a performance, an imitation with or without origin, and corporeality is provisional upon its modes of realization.[37]

Even though Papadat-Bengescu concentrates on intermingling the two concepts of gender and class as they are played out on the characters, she focuses primarily on the representation of gender that provides the impetus to the narrative action in the form of the feminine protagonists. Functioning as a multiplicity of performed identities reflected by a range of other characters who challenge the nature of gender and show it to be a performance, the bodies of Lenora, Coca-Aimée, and Elena may well be one and the same person in the discourse about gender, in the sense that the irreducible physicality of their bodies is linked to the structure of the text. Thus their bodies emerge as more than a pure physical and material entity; rather, they are also imagined and represented ones, provisional constructions that entail different understandings of representation, subjectivity and identity, and give further credence to the thoroughly modern young woman's comment in *Heartbreak House* that "the soul is the body, and the body of the soul".[38] Thus the body becomes the modality of expression emblematic of shifts in cultural sensibility, understood as modes of apprehension and representation. Ultimately, Papadat-

Bengescu's emphasis on her feminine characters' bodies in their social and sexual modalities reflects her understanding of women's bodies "not as a given but as a changing horizon of multiple becomings."[39]

Giving authority to sexual desire and to the experiential body, Lenora is a former nymph with a sensuous body, whose symptoms of neurasthenia and developing phases of uterine cancer show the submissive role of women and reinforce their inferiority to men. While her neurasthenia is a sign of displacement and psychological damage, a site of communicability that inscribes and makes visible physically the way in which society deforms women, her ovarian cancer illness illustrates both the idea made popular by Schopenhauer that the "disease fits the character" (of the patient) and the notion that "disease expresses character" (126).[40] As her battle with cancer makes a shift in emphasis away from the authenticity of her body as a source and site of identity, her cancer acts as (1) a metaphor of Lenora's outsider status in the marriage to Doctor Walter; and (2) a performance of her damaged femininity and subsequent marginalization in the Barodin Palace, another sign that she has fitted in, and been damaged as a result. Thus, if Lenora's sexuality and fertility reflect her strategy as a woman, her cancer is a sign representative of an untouchable, unrepresentable trauma presenting her body not as a given but as a process of embodiment that necessarily references representational practices. In speaking about his cancer-stricken wife, Doctor Walter points out accusingly that she is the only one to blame. She had been concealing it [the cancer] slyly and obstinate, out of ignorance, coquetry, shame of that given infirmity by which she felt dishonored. What was left of her former slyness was just enough to prevent her from giving away the secret of her disqualification as a female (122).

With the recurrence of the cancer after the surgery, Lenora suffers silently in her bed at the Walter Sanatorium. Under the care of young Doctor Pejan, Doctor Walter's assistant, she is aware that her illness makes visible on a physical level the system of marginalization and exclusion by which a patriarchal society operates:

> Lenora grieved; bleak premonitions concerning her disease emerged from the depths of her body. She turned to the wall, tightening the cover around her body like a shroud; she closed her eyes, looking into the dark behind her eyelids to see something frightening. She felt disqualified in front of Walter, of Pejan, of all the men in the world, as she had ceased being intact as a woman. (137)

If Papadat-Bengescu's portrayal of Lenora brings forth the embedded themes of sexuality and women as wives and mothers, her depiction of Coca-Aimée is a feminist rewriting that challenges the ideas of patriarchy and offers alternative paths for the young protagonist. Specifically, if Lenora exhibits sexuality and fertility as a woman's strategy under patriarchal discourse, in Coca-Aimée's case the emphasis is on the staging of her character's body as a scenario that attains its meaning through its position and transposition in the modality of a script adapted to a specific cultural and social context. At the core of her character's portrayal is Coca-Aimée's shift from her mother's position as a woman within patriarchal discourse to a deliberate mimicry achieved through the subversive strategy of woman under patriarchal discourse. Defined by Luce Irigaray as "a theatrical staging of the mime: miming the miming imposed on woman,"[41] the deliberate mimicry that Coca-Aimée performs is a stance best captured in Doctor Walter's initial observation that Lenora and Coca-Aimée "resembled each other like a double copy that now accompanied him everywhere" (29). Substantiating Toril Moi's view that such mimicry "intends to undo the effects of phallocentric discourse simply by overdoing them,"[42] Coca-Aimée is a doll who not only mimics Lenora's seductive beauty, but also takes it to perfection with

> her white rosy skin as if made of porcelain; pale-colored majolica-pink lips; large, Delft blue eyes as in certain types of lithographs; blonde eyebrows thinly drawn as if by a fine brush on a straight forehead; an admirable oval face. A doll without any character or expression in its beauty, yet perfect and outstanding, especially by the quality of the materials nature had used: silk, color, everything first rate, with no defect in texture. (320)

Simultaneously lewd and virginal, Coca-Aimée represents both perverse infantile desire and socially conditioned and repressed adult desire. The combined pressures of social convention and the masculine gaze on Coca-Aimée are evident both in her relations with Doctor Walter, when she assumes a child-like fragility and innocence, and in her frequent outings in the elegant Rolls and visits at the club or the horse racing track when she pursues vicious and dangerous infatuations. Distracted by her own pleasure and obsessive devotion to selfish occupations, Coca-Aimée's character seems to declare that there is no longer one representation of her body but that her body may offer a multi-discursive array of intrusions through and into the conventions of representation. She feels at ease in Bucharest, the Living City, with its crowds, its chaos, its drunkards, and even its threatening women like Cora Perşu and other regulars of the Sports Club where the fragmented nature of her psyche, which rests upon the interconnected breakdown of her parents' marriage, prompts Coca-Aimée's move towards performance and theatricality. At all times "hermetically sealed in self-idolatry" (308), she drifts into moments of performative exaggeration, which are all the more powerful in the face of the hegemonic patriarchal discourse because they are entirely staged and deliberately miming. Her habit of calling her mother "Mamile" and her child-like stammering speech are the ways in which Coca-Aimée deforms the language, a process in line with Irigaray's views that "woman as mimic stages her own exclusion from patriarchal discourse in her language of physical symptoms and mimicry of verbal language."[43]

With her voice heard in the blank spaces between words, in the gaps of the text, Coca-Aimée is an outsider to hegemonic patriarchal discourse who also deforms her body and appearance. As hostess in the Barodin Palace, she is

> dressed up at evening balls in lavish, gold-embroidered brocade dresses, tailored after stylish patterns and brushing the parquet floors, and her artificial-looking blonde hair required cinema-like diadems. In this way, certain hard-to-launch outfits had found in Aimée a suitable mannequin and a buyer. In search of originality, Aimée would courageously wear the heavy folds of ten meters of expensive cloth. On her first appearance, the girl's dress became the matter of gossip in the evening's chatter. (378)

Playing on the theatricality of her performance, Coca-Aimée's dresses are reminiscent of the artificial trappings of femininity and of the emphasis on fakery. In choosing to wear such elaborate outfits, Aimée transforms her own life into a fairy tale, deliberately and consciously adopting a series of roles for which children's literature and fashion magazines provide the template. Overwhelmed by "the voluptuous congestion of triumph," Doctor Walter himself watches in the elegant reception hall of his palace "the figure of the girl often turned up within the frame of this landscape: the little hostess was there performing her duty, strengthening the reality of things and at the same time feeding the fairy tale of life" (378).

The danger in Coca-Aimée's submission to social codes, a type of surrender that suggests that her body may become reified through social practices, so that she is ultimately redefined in terms of the submission, control, and instrumentalization of her body, is challenged in Cora Perşu's explanations

> that the feminine mystery neither resided nor disappeared in the folds of dresses – that the mystery would find shelter anywhere, be it in the transparent veil of Daphne, or merely in the metallic belt of the naked belly dancer. Cora was leaving enough room for others to think or feel that the mystery could equally well be concealed

> in the masculine-looking waistcoat of a woman's much too severe costume. At those balls, Cora wore a tight black velvet dress, rather long and very low cut on a perfect but lifeless bust. (378)

The theatricality of embodiment, which allows Coca-Aimée to assume fake identities that postpone consolidation into a body, becomes for Cora Perşu the freedom of occupying different gender positions at the same time or of taking on different sexual roles. With a body "too thin, no hips, no breasts" (337), and an initial contempt for men coupled with an attraction for Coca-Aimée, Cora's character attests to Papadat-Bengescu's understanding of sexual difference that is not foundational, but merely the effect of representation defined as a play of resemblances. Later on, when Cora distances herself from Coca-Aimée and appears on the arm of previously absent fiancé in a stance that triggers Doctor Walter's admiration for her beauty, Cora's character inscribes the mark of reversibility not between the sexes, but within sexuality, by acknowledging that the ostensibly deceptive or illusionistic effects of representation reflect the traces of contingency and defer essentialist consolidations.

The representation of sexuality, that is, of sexuality not constituted nominally in an existentialist mode, but dialogically, as performance, reaches its climactic point in the decisive confrontation between Coca-Aimée and Doctor Walter. The scene, which engages Doctor Walter (who is writing a letter to Hilda Gert) and Coca-Aimée (who attempts to read the letter without suspecting that the Doctor is watching her) casts the two protagonists in a reversed sexual mold: their actions and attitudes do not rely upon the enforced polarity between the sexes but on the potential reversibility of their roles.

Filled with emotion, hesitant in choosing his words, trying even to address the young woman in her native German, and baring his soul, Doctor Walter displays a soft and feminine eloquence as he attempts to write: "*Liebe Freundin ...beide ... zusammengefuhlt*" and again, on a different piece of paper, "Miss Hilda! It's been several weeks since I wanted to write to you. But this letter is not the one ..." (486). Infusing a contrasting a forceful male sexuality into this narrative texture, Coca-Aimée reads the letter and becomes filled with contempt for Doctor Walter's weakness and feeling that she "could have crushed Hilda like a fly" (486). Her attitude, which is an ostensible affirmation and display of a vigorous and virile style, allows for further weaving of sexuality within the fabric of the text when Doctor Walter, who is "caressing with his warm fingers the cold polish of a slim fragile onyx column supporting the raw head of a Cupid" (488), watches Coca-Aimée read and put away the letter that she calculates to be to her advantage. Suggestive of the Doctor's inherent weakness and even the threat of impotence, insinuated again, later on, in his "small thrill of repulsion at thought of her [Coca-Aimée's] virginity" (502), this scene reveals the rhetorical manipulation and transposition of sexuality into the language of Papadat-Bengescu's narrative. By conventional sexual roles, insofar as the male is presented as active and the female as passive or receptive, Doctor Walter's silent and motionless gaze and Coca-Aimée's determined actions point to a narrative texture that mixes allusions to both sexes. When Coca-Aimée's limpid blue eyes meet in the darkness of the office "Doctor Walter's golden eyes that seemed more metallic than ever" (489), the text becomes the allegorical emblem of a mold where masculinity and femininity are cast as reversible forms. At the end of the encounter, Coca-Aimée's mind and body and their embodiments in the interplay with Doctor Walter's redefine patriarchal paradigms through which femininity and masculinity achieve their new conceptual and material realization:

> Her [Coca-Aimée's] sentiments were calm and limpid, a chemical analysis of them would have proved nothing but dubious. Only the labels on the flasks of social conventions annoyed her and called for precautions. She decided it was time to go to sleep.
>
> Back in the office, Walter was left disappointed and confused. In his present uncertainty, he was wondering what attitude he should assume in relation to Aimée. Had she seen him? Had he seen her? Her innocent exit, however, mixed up in the threads. What was he going to say and do the next day? (490)

Once again, the reversibility that Papadat-Bengescu ascribes to the two sexes is not to be understood as a denial of sexual difference. Rather it indicates a reconceptualization of sexuality by which the meaning of sexuality emerges as marked by intersexual overtones.

In spite of occasional submission to social codes suggested on a physical plane by her "hemorrhagic complexion" (488) and "warm waves of blood that flowed" (484) indicating her womanly condition, Coca-Aimée opens up her body to the revalorization of experience. The traumatic scene in which she loses her virginity, "the miserable pains she has suffered" (466) followed by her confused and disorderly run through the raging storm, echoes a version of the original sin and the price of knowledge, further suggesting a form of feminine authenticity and of subjecthood. The violent sexual encounter and subsequent illness emphasize her body as an organ of experience and points to her radical redefinition – to Coca-Aimée's transformation from merely the beautiful object Doctor Walter desires for his collection into an embodied subject that reminds us how, in Virginia Woolf's words, "All day, all night the body intervenes."[44]

Unlike Hilda Gert, whose honesty, "obliging and obedient nature" (451), and immense capacity for love and devotion mark her as one of the most praiseworthy female types that reinforces male hegemony through her demure behavior, Coca-Aimée engages in a ritual reenactment of the banishment of domestic tradition up to the point at which she contemplates how she will cheat, "cautiously, of course" (504), on Doctor Walter, her future husband. Although "a creature of porcelain and silk," she will prove "a trinket both more fragile and more resilient than the ones [Doctor Walter] had in the Barodin Palace; an object of art one could not molest and which kept its distance" (310). Proving to be completely different from the virtuous, German-born Hilda,[45] Coca-Aimée reverses traditional patterns of women's victimization by positing an alternative strategy for expressing female subjectivity other than suffering: laughter.

> She did hate Hilda fiercely, murderously. Walter's letter was a defeat for her, but she wouldn't take it into account. She would only take into account her victory, of which that same letter was also a record. ... She ignored his shriveled face and metallic eyes in order to imagine him as a ridiculous hero of a German idyll with a governess! How stupid! She laughed, and the laughter triggered a small loss of blood; she stiffened her body even more. (489-90)

Manifested by the body as physical gesture, laughter represents a form of opposition, an act of rebellion against patriarchal control. Rooted in the body, Coca-Aimée's laughter represents her potential to resist, subvert, and undermine conformity to a male-dominated culture and environment.

Although some critics have argued that Coca-Aimée and Doctor Walter are complementary characters, with matching and reversible characterstics,[46] the character who possesses in equal share with Doctor Walter excessive pride, arrogance, and calculated ambition regardless of the moral cost is Elena Drăgănescu, the object of Coca-Aimée's occasional envy. Doctor Walter himself notices his similarity with Elena when he thinks that "on a sort of graded scale ... the two of them were two top exemplars" (498). Although less aware on an intermediate level of their similarity, Elena too comments on the Walter Sanatorium, whose splendor matches that of her own mansion on the Lascăr Catargiu Boulevard. Her conclusion that "the man was victoriously being driven ahead by a real vocation. The stairs of that sumptuous house were the steps of a hidden way, more powerful than reason" (501) reveals a deep understanding of Doctor Walter's social ambition that she alone can fathom.

Like Doctor Walter's marriage to Lenora, Elena's marriage to Drăgănescu is also governed by convention and social contract, a transaction or an exchange based on mutual obligations.

With the move to the city after her marriage to the wealthy but feeble financier, and after the birth of their son, Elena's sexuality blossoms while she is undergoing considerable and elaborate changes, from a "simple and silent girl with chestnut hair" to the elegant hostess "presiding over all of Bucharest" (320). Here, in the city, Elena's life forbids the rituals of domestic duties and replaces them with the new "business" of servants, fashion, furnishings, and elegant gatherings, like the famous musical soirée featuring the virtuoso magician Marcian that seals Elena's marriage to Drăgănescu. Her attraction to Marcian, detailed in A *Concert of Music by Bach*, turns her body into a mode of expression that brings into relief an understanding of the body as a representational and experiential entity. Affected by the musical performance that brings into it the realm of physical expression, the previously fixed, inert, and voiceless entity that was Elena's body becomes a site for a mediated exercise, attuned to the particular tones of Marcian's music.

The physicality of Elena's character as reflected in her "admirable bearing, the simple gravity of her complexion, the smooth outline of her somber silhouette, the pure line of her profile," is an expression of her embodiedness at its most extreme; she is, in Doctor Walter's estimation, "the best exemplar of the family" (497). Her name plays on her identification with a mythical figure, the beautiful Helen, and her elegant body, speaking not as a single voice, but as the sound of two lovers' dialogue, signifies the gratifying power of a woman's love. If Salema and later Lenora "clear the way of obstacles" (496) for Doctor Walter, Drăgănescu's unexpected death makes possible Elena's union with Marcian. As Doctor Walter remarks with knowing appreciation, for Elena "even the sudden blows of fate seem to serve that woman favorably. For her everything was always both correct and profitable at the same time" (493).

To Coca-Aimée, who is jealous of her sister, Elena is "free and rich" (495) and "so successful in everything she tries" (468). As "the prototype of the winning woman,"47 Elena is so perfect in her mourning moment shared with Coca-Aimée that she makes Doctor Walter stir with the collector's desire: "side by side, the two sisters were making up a new funerary fresco. It seemed to him that an artistic bas-relief was being added to his collection" (499). But if Doctor Walter can "marry Coca-Aimée in order to make her available for the cause, built, like the other two [Salema and Lenora], into the walls of the abbey of his own ambition" (503), Elena will escape this fate. Unlike Coca-Aimée, who ultimately validates the patriarchal notion that a woman's status and desirability rest on whether she is pretty, Elena is strong and self-assured. More important, unlike

Doctor Walter, Elena understands the relationship between sexuality and the imagination, its mythic character also inherent in her name.

As an experience proper to the expression of the body, the experience of sexual pleasure defines Elena's relation with Marcian and accounts for what Doctor Walter calls her "harmonious destiny" (498). By contrast, Doctor Walter's recompenses, the Barodin Palace, his highly privileged social status consolidated through the projected marriage with Coca-Aimée, the "object of art [that] had to be set for good among his collection" (488), and even his art collection, do not come with the currency of sexual pleasure in love. It is in this sense that his inner yearning for an ever higher personal satisfaction, could not be offered him in the end. Pleasure derived simply out of possession, rather than reciprocity which love alone can give as payment in kind, is an act of defilement that reduces the body to an inanimate object, the self that Doctor Walter will ultimately incorporate in his art collection.

In the final analysis, Doctor Walter's exclusion of the female body in his marriage to Lenora coincides with the more radical erasure of his physical body. If antiques and art objects can replace physical needs and enjoyment, it is because Doctor Walter's body has no meaning in and of itself, other than as the embodiment of his social ambitions and exigencies.

The erasure of Doctor Walter's body involves Papadat-Bengescu's clever conceit upon which the presence of the female body inscribes itself as the mediating and ultimately prevailing force particularly suited to the writer's type of feminist revision. Thus, the assertion of the female body in *The Hidden Way* marks both the extinction of a system that relied on a disenfranchisement of the female in the traditionally patriarchal Romanian society and the new, revisionist proclamation of the female body as the legitimate medium for the transmission of power and fulfillment. In this context, Lenora can in the end appropriate her daughter, Coca-Aimée, as an extension of her own being while at the same time overlooking paternity in the system of social reproduction; Coca-Aimée may feel perfectly at ease in thinking about Doctor Walter as a man "of no importance at all" and "a capture" (489) for her purposes; and Elena's erasure of Drăgănescu as her husband and father of her son, who prefers his mother's lover, "*ami* Vic," over his own father, the faraway "Papa Bucharest," may well be construed to suggest a crisis or, rather, a rejection of patrilineal legitimacy. In a narrative discourse that reclaims the writing of woman's body, *The Hidden Way*, as well as the previous novels of the Hallipa trilogy, inscribes a reversal of the disenfranchisement of the female in the patriarchal tradition and exploits the identification of woman and body as means of writing back through and with the body in practices of Cixousian *écriture avant la lettre*.

CHAPTER 4

Mapping Orality and Literacy in Romanian Modern Fiction: Mihail Sadoveanu's *The Hatchet* and *Tales From Ancuța's Inn*

> While other literatures profited from the styles of Classicism and the Renaissance, Romanian literature, without remaining free of the impulses from Athens, Byzantium and Rome, roseupon the generous foundation of folklore and grew primarily out of its substance. [...] Folklore basically generated a marked classical character [...] thus proving Lessing's opinion (in *Laokoon*) that, in their stages as a young culture, all people spontaneously follow the principles of classical beauty. (Constantin Ciopraga, *The Personality of Romanian Literature*, 23)

In *Orality and Literacy* Walter Ong describes "orality and literacy as two rigidly differentiated entities"[1] thus foreclosing the possibility of a conceptual middle ground. Although such a binary model establishing a great cognitive divide has been challenged in post-Ongian scholarship, which recognizes that "in most societies there is an overlap and a 'mix' of [oral and literate] modes of communication,"[2] the quality, content and form of storytelling vis-à-vis a fusion of orality and literacy have not wholly been addressed in the case of specific national narratives.

By postulating two epistemic systems, one oral and the other literate, this essay proposes to examine the literate episteme not as the polar opposite of the oral episteme but as a union and evidence of a single, harmonious discourse that has emerged in Romanian literature from the human capacity to depart from a particular way of knowing. As I intend to demonstrate, oral (generated through voice) and literate (articulated through the written word) cultures have collectively generated in Romanian fiction "an increasingly articulated introspectivity – " one, indeed, that allows the fictional psyche to open "as never before not only to the external objective world quite distinct from itself but also to the interior self against whom the objective world is set" (Ong, *Orality*, 105). Finally, my purpose is to show that since the 1800s, when the magazine *Dacia literară* (Literary Dacia) called for original literary works inspired by a largely oral folk culture, Romanian literature began turning consistently toward ballads, tales, and legends rooted in rural communities and circulated through oral tradition, and focused on transforming them into literary themes and mythic archetypes that captured the cultural landscape in the new configurations of high literature.

Relying on the example of the nineteenth century when all great Romanian writers and poets, from the revered poet Mihail Eminescu onward, integrated in their work folk values and oral creations, twentieth-century literary critics, beginning with Nicolae Iorga, were united in asserting that folk (oral) culture played an essential role in the genesis of a national Romanian literature.[3] Even literary luminaries like Emil Cioran, who had taken the path of exile to France, professed attachment to the folk-inspired culture of their native country. In what may be considered a eulogy to his adoptive Paris, Cioran stated:

> I did not insult you by thinking of another homeland, I did not abase myself for seeking ecstasy in my roots or in the nostalgias of blood. I silenced in my blood the rumblings of generations of plowmen bent over the stilt and no lament of a Danube peasant comes to trouble the minuet of doubt that your clouds are dancing. I folded the pride of my wanderings into your absence of homeland, and my despair – hymn against time – adorns itself with a bloodied halo. (93)[4]

Continuing this cultural model in the more recent, Communist era of the second half of the twentieth century, critics like Ion Dodu Bălan emphasized once again the notion of an organic Romanian literature nourished by folk traditions. In his *Concise History of Romanian Literature*, Bălan points out that, "for several centuries, the Romanians' specific artistic and literary expression that have survived all hardship were embodied in folk art and folklore, crystallizing the essential elements of Romanian spirituality, and subsequently handed down to the cultured arts and literature."[5] Bălan's claim, shared by other critics like Ciopraga, (see the epigraph), argued that Romanian folklore "held the place of humanism and classicism" during the earlier times (8).[6]

Valorizing to the highest degree the epic potential of folk ballads, folk motifs and typology, Mihail Sadoveanu's novels *The Hatchet* (1930) and *Tales from Ancuța's Inn* (1928) move from the tangible orality of Romanian folklore to the conceptualizing lenses of literacy contoured by their engagement with the written word, and thus prohibit any possibility of categorizing these systems as exclusive. Quite to the contrary, the oral epistemes of the ballad *Miorița* (The Ewe Lamb) and of the folk types and core beliefs of a primitive Romanian culture emerge in *The Hatchet* and *Tales from Ancuța's Inn* as fundamental and inextricable elements n the shaping of and engagement with the literate epistemes of Sadoveanu's novels.

The numerous characteristics of orally sustainable thought present in these two narratives include, among others, a strong disposition toward conservation of Romanian cultural values and traditionalism focused on the preservation of the status quo, a fulfillment of readers' expectations that forecloses ambivalent or open endings, and a collective social orientation that encourages imitative and redundant structures with no concept of plagiarism. In this context, the interface between highly literate narration and orally inflected texts can be mapped directly onto the two novels' narrative configuration that features the interpenetration and recycling of an oral episteme, the *Mioriţa* ballad.

With its mystic structure, submissive rhetoric and minimal narrative, *Mioriţa* is Romania's most enduring cultural text. In *Destinul culturii romîneşti* (*The Fate of Romanian Culture*), Mircea Eliade states that Romania has only two legends of its own, *Mioriţa* and *Master Builder Manole*, each preserved in "lyrical and ballad masterpieces" (25).[7] Of the two, Eliade singles out *Mioriţa* as a piece that belongs most specifically to Romania, since the *Master Builder Manole* legend also has variants throughout the Balkan region, in Macedonia, Bulgaria, and Greece and possible origins in the Thracian myth of Orpheus. In "*The Mioriţa*: An Introduction in the Form of a Memoir," Ernest H. Latham describes the *Mioriţa* "as the great defining ballad of the Romanian personality and culture, ranking in Romanian self-consciousness with the *Iliad* and the *Odyssey* for the Greeks, *Beowulf* for the Anglo-Saxons, the *Lay of the Host of Igor* for the Russians, the *Ballad of Kosovo* for the Serbs, *El Cid* for the Spanish, or the *Nibelungenlied* for the Germans."[8]

Viewed against the background of folk tradition, Sadoveanu's *The Hatchet*[9] captures the genius of folk culture, whose elemental forces determine the novel's system of images and artistic outlook on the world. Told and retold in countless versions, usually of about 123 short lines, *Mioriţa* is a nostalgic, lyrical tragic story of a shepherd murdered by his traveling companions, two other shepherds who envy his wealth and kill him so that they can take ownership of his sheep. Even though he is forewarned by his beloved ewe lamb that he will be killed, the young shepherd accepts his destiny unquestioningly and begs the faithful ewe lamb to tell the other two shepherds to have him buried in the meadows near his sheep, so that he may be close to his beloved woods, the birds and the stars. He then asks the ewe lamb to urge everyone not to speak of his death but rather to tell everyone – especially his teary-eyed mother who will be looking for him – that he married a prince's daughter at heaven's gate.

In a country long troubled by external conquerors and internal conflicts like Romania, the ballad *Mioriţa* may be well understood as a primeval myth infused with the pastoral origin of the Romanian people, as well as the drama of its cosmic destiny. Having to take refuge from the threats presented to the country's borders by escaping to its mountains and forests. Romanians are close to a nature they consider a sanctuary. According to Mircea Eliade, the Romanian spirit is rooted in a mystical existence of reunion with nature and its contemplation, a condition which entails disregarding or ignoring history's temporal dimensions, but remaining conscious of one's own spiritual eternity. In his study *Zamolxis, the Vanishing God*,[10] Eliade sees the shepherd's acceptance of death in the Mioriţa ballad not as a capitulation but rather as an acknowledgement of higher cosmic laws: the shepherd converts his imminent death into a mystical reunion with a cosmic world, a magic wedding that gives meaning to an incomprehensible historical destiny. Expanding on the philosophical dimensions of the *Mioriţa* ballad, Lucien Blaga, one of Romania's greatest poets and philosophers, defines in *Spaţiul Mioritic* (*Undulated Space, 1923*)[11] the concept of the Mioritic space as delineating the specific geography of the Romanian poetic imagination and as a national archetypal style expressing the Romanian ethos of resignation in the face of an oppressive historical destiny. As one recent historian of the Romanians, Vlad Georgescu summarizes it, *Mioriţa* is "a philosophical attempt to explain the Romanian spirit through the Romanian landscape, which Lucian Blaga saw as the stylistic matrix of Romanian culture."[12]

Turning the ballad's rhythmical pattern into a crisp prose style, *The Hatchet* reconstructs the centuries' old *Mioriţa* in the novel's plot as it tells the story of Nechifor Lipan, a well-to-do shepherd from the village of Măgura, who is murdered by two other shepherds, Ilie Cuţui and Calistrat Bogza, while the three men are journeying together toward the land where Nechifor wishes to leave his sheep for the winter. In Sadoveanu's story, however, Nechifor Lipan is the victim of a wicked plot and unexpectedly struck by the murderer, Calistrat Bogza, with a hatchet, from the back, while the other shepherd, Ilie Cuţui, is keeping watch. Nechifor's body is then left to rot underneath a mountain ravine, prey to wild beasts and sinister ravens.[13]

Worried that her husband is not returning home as he usually does after selling his sheep or taking them to warmer lands for the winter, Nechifor's wife, Vitoria, decides to leave their home village of Măgura high up in the mountains to look for him. Accompanied by her son, Gheorghiţă, she plans to trace Nechifor's steps, as she is reasonably sure, in spite of the assurances of the village priest, that her husband is long dead, murdered by the thieves whom she wishes brought to justice. *The Hatchet* is thus her story, from the moment when she embarks on the long journey at the beginning of spring to the moment when she cleverly identifies both her husband's murderer and his accomplice, far away from her village home but near the very site of the heinous crime that she manages to piece together ingeniously more than a year later.

Although it does not borrow its storyline from the *Mioriţa*, *Tales From Ancuţa's Inn*[14] also articulates in its narrative space the *Mioriţa* ballad. Played during a stop at the inn by a traveling blind beggar on his bagpipes, the sorrowful tune of the *Mioriţa* ballad provides yet another aspect of the cultural dimension of orality. Serving this time as a document of the Romanian people's national identity, the ballad is used here as a multicultural property of the Romanians from the historically divided provinces, who are represented in the ballad's verses by the three shepherd-protagonists: one is a Moldavian, the other a Wallachian (Vrâncean), and the third a Transylvanian (Ungurean).[15] While accommodating regionally specific accounts, this adaptation of the *Miorița* retains common narrative elements with other versions, such as the minimal action plot, superficial psychological representation of the murdered shepherd's passive attitude towards his own death, and the certain symbolic attributes and characteristics of Romanian morality, philosophy and artistic sensibility that allows a crosscultural recognition of the tale in all Romanian communities.[16] As a testimony to the ballad's strong cultural appeal, when the blind beggar sings the *Miorița*, all the travelers at the inn listen in rapture to its melancholy tune, which is to them a moving emotional experience and one that is being renewed with every chance they get to hear it.

Since, as Benedict Anderson has pointed out, European nations were created around well-known myths and legends, like those of Roland, Boadicea, Vercingetorix, etc.,[17] the narratives told in the *Tales*, like the *Miorița* ballad, stem from a narrative consciousness which in turn confers a sociological solidity upon the iconographic characters of the *Tales*. Each of the storytellers seeking shelter and merriment at Ancuța's Inn portrays in turn a protagonist firmly entrenched in a specific social milieu – a village, a small town, the Prince's court, etc. – that provides an analogous construct for both the narrative world of the inn and the symbolic space of the inn signifying the nation. Indeed, although the narrative matrix of the stories presents a veritable *tour d'horizon*, it does not offer *un tour du monde*. Drawing on folk stories that tem from a collective past and portray iconographic characters, the stories told at the inn form a homogenized amalgam, an imagined community that corresponds to Herder's notion of *Volk* and is analogous to the process of the building of the nation through myth-making and fabulation.

From the very beginning, the opening lines that describe the inn and its surroundings echo the specific tendency of the Romanian oral folk tales to treat the fantastic "realistically, with great deal of rural local color:"[18]

ONE golden autumn I heard many a tale at Ancuța's Inn. But that was long ago, during the year in which such awful rains fell on St. Elijah's Day that people said that they had seen a black dragon up in the clouds over the overflowing water of the Moldova River. They also saw some birds, the like of which had never before been seen, whirl in the storm and sail towards the East. And Moş Leonte, consulting his almanac and explaining the signs of the Emperor Heraclitus, showed that these birds, whose feathers were the color of frost, had been borne hither by the winds that rose from the islands at the edge of the Earth and foretold war between Empires, as well as an abundant grape harvest.

And the White Emperor did indeed throw his Muscovites against the pagan world, and, that the stars should fulfill their prophecies, God gave such abundant crops to the vineyards of Lower Moldavia that the vintners didn't have enough barrels for their wine, and the carters from our parts set out to bring the wine to the mountains. Then came the time for revelry and story-telling at Ancuţa's Inn. (19)

As travelers' and locals' "convoys of carts rumble along outside incessantly […] true masters roast[ed] choice cuts of ram and veal, or grill[ed] fish fresh from the Moldova River […] and folk musicians played and sang inside ceaselessly […] and the men drinking smashed so many mugs and jugs," men gather to tell stories associated with ethnographic epics or factual events, current or past. The oldest of the travelers stopped at the inn, the astrologer *Moş* Leonte,[19] gives the following account:

Ever since I could remember, from the time of the Ancuţa of the past, we, in these parts, have been used to sitting and talking things over, paying homage to the wine of the South at the same time. And while enjoying this most excellent drink, we listen to stories of the past. In my opinion, […] there isn't another inn like this to be found anywhere, no matter how much you'd travel the Earth. (36-37)

The stories are precisely delineated and, in spite of the differences in tone and narrative register, they affirm an ethnically and culturally identifiable space and a collective portrait of the Romanian community. In this sense, the *Tales* reaffirms the notion that, beyond political and economic considerations, a nation recommends itself through processes of cultural identification that hold a people together and enable it to survive through storytelling. Identifying themselves with the Romanian people, the travelers at the inn foreground in their stories a performative discourse whose oral inflections mix folkloric realism with gothic fantasy and archaic myth with the actuality of the raconteurs' own time. As the storytelling experience unfolds itself, in keeping with orally inflected participation, the travelers comment publicly on the narrative as it proceeds and then show signs of engagement through a respectful silence. And so, oral articulations give way to spectatorial quietude, to a reverential silence that allows for the meditative distance required to obtain the emerging engagement with a literately inflected text and the overarching discourse.

Orality helps explain why characters in both *The Hatchet* and *Tales* are flat and amplified mainly from a visual, frontal perspective. In a photograph-like portrait, Vitoria Lipan appears with "her hazel eyes, in which the chestnut glint of her hair seemed to be reflected, held a faraway look. The spindle [in her hands] spun diligently as of its own accord […] Engulfed as in the darkness of night, her keen, still youthful eyes continued to scan the unexplored horizon"(5). With his "black moustache, those eyes with slanting eyebrows, [and] his squarely-built, broad-shouldered figure" (6) her husband, Nechifor, seems another embodiment frozen in time of the doomed shepherd in the *Miorița* ballad smiling melancholy upon us from a faraway realm.

Similarly, in *Tales* the structuring of the narrative around the travelers' portraits satisfies a primitive set of aesthetic expectations suited to the time and location of the stories and storytelling. Like wall paintings found on the walls of Moldova's painted monasteries, the storytellers direct the readers' gaze outward to the created world (of which they come to form a part) and not inward to their individual psyche. The unity of the *Tales* is built upon the assembled company of travelers, with the narrator actually a part of the social order that he describes and a means for the reader of entry into it. Once inside, the reader can easily recognize each of the travelers at the inn from the description which relates to their countenance and their identifiable attire: the Merchant who "wore a fur cap and coat and [whose] beard was tidy, neatly cut and rounded with scissors … beaming all over his full and jovial face – the face of a man who had always eaten plentifully" (91); the blind beggar, "with his expressionless face, framed in its wild beard, [and] dressed like a mountain-dweller, with a little black hat, the white costume of his people, and a sheepskin cloak clasped only at the shoulder" (103); or the unforgettable Captain Isac, "with a swarthy face, a short mustache and a rounded beard, an aquiline nose and dark eyebrows that still held the traces of virile beauty, although his right cheek was crumpled under the dry eye-socket permanently set in a mask of agony, while his live eye, large and dark, merely stared down into the black well of the past; he wore high boots of Russian leather and a tunic of blue woolen cloth with round silver buttons, held at this side a yellow leather bag, and there were pistols in his holster" (48-9). In both works actions are outwardly oriented and housed in a Manichaean universe in which ritual, inflated violence and melodrama occupy center stage.

In *The Hatchet*, where such manifestations abound, when Nechifor is found, the degradation suffered by his body hurled into the void of the ravine by the murderers and his roaming spirit "risen every night to his feet, clad in the rug" (95) must be transformed into regenerating value and overcome through ritual into a new birth. At the murder site and during the burial, folk tradition dictates the need to set right the dead man's impious end and to glorify the deceased.

After being removed from the ravine, Nechifor's bones are sanctified through the funeral rites. That process, which includes strong elements of dramatic display, such as the washing of the bones, the crying of the hired mourners, and the priests' sprinkling of the bones with holy water, resembles an elaborate spectacle, with specific roles to be performed by all participants, from the widow to the mourners.

Marking the final moment in the ritual of the dead, the commemorative feast Vitoria gives immediately after the funeral service, celebrates Nechifor's luminous memory and his cosmic transformation into an incandescent, positive force in afterlife – something not that much different from the celestial glory the young slain shepherd in the *Miorița* ballad envisions for himself when he asks the little ewe lamb to present his death to his mother as a wedding to a heavenly princess. By contrast with the glorified deceased, the two murderers, Calistrat Bogza and Ilie Cuțui, degrade the ceremonial and ensuing feast through their mere physical presence. Added to their excessive drinking, their appearance – one "of a small build and swarthy, the other burlier and with a harelip" (69) – conveys their grotesque,[20] debased, and alienating characters defined by a vulgar sense of their recently accumulated wealth stolen from the deceased. Seated toward the lower end of the huge table, the two appear severed from the other guests, as blunt and reprehensible as their flippant conversation. In their humiliating isolation, Calistrat Bogza and Ilie Cutui are coarse and deadly obstacles to the collective celebration and their presence is seen as the element of negation, breaking the continually renewed link with a cosmic regenerating force. In the end, Calistrat Bogza, the murderer of Vitoria's husband, is killed by Nechifor Lipan's own dog that attacks and bites him mortally. While bleeding to death, Cuțui makes a dramatic, public confession of his crime and expresses his admiration for Vitoria's ingenious investigation.

In Sadoveanu's vision, the travelers stopping at Ancuța's Inn are the ones best able to judge occurrences from the past and to become alarmed at the prospect of a threat to social well-being and justice. It is there, in their midst, that the terms of social inclusion or exclusion are formulated, with the tales acting as an argument and criteria for the selection process. Stories of inclusiveness take account of persecuted lovers like the young *mazâl* and Aglăița, the *boyar*'s daughter in "The Tale of Zaharia the Water Witch," or the bold Todiriță Cătană and the Lady Varvara in "The Other Ancuța;" and of outlaws who defend the lowly and the helpless, like the thief Vasile the Great and the suffering peasant in "Justice of the Poor." Other tales argue for the exclusion of evil rulers like Duca-Vodă ("The Blind Beggar's Tale"), cruel and greedy high ranking officials like Costeau Căruntu ("The Other Ancuța"), wicked and depraved *boieri* like Răducan Chioru ("Justice of the Poor"), or Nătase Bolomir ("The Dragon"); and heartless gypsies like the old man Hasanache who murder their own for immediate gain ("The Well Among the Poplars").

Amalgamated in the text of the *Tales* are characters like Todiriță Cătană or Vasile the Great who illustrate folk typology specific of the Danubian region, like the *haiduk* featured into the folk and high literature.[21] Reenacting ancestral myths of Romanian folk poems that feature the primitive motif of what George Călinescu calls "the invasion of erotic instinct" (Călinescu, *Istoria* 65), some of the stories told in the *Tales* foreground violent sexuality turned into high romance material, as in the beautifully crafted love stories of Lady Varvara ("The Other Ancuța), the tragic gypsy girl Magda whose body is thrown into a well as punishment for forbidden love ("The Well Among the Poplars"), or the privileged young girl Aglaiță whose love for an unsuitable poor peasant ends on a happy note thanks to the intervention of a shrewd water witch.

Linked to orality as they are to elementariness, Sadoveanu's narratives highlight dialogic excess and draw attention to the highly visual, flat spectacle. In *Tales*, the travelers at Ancuța's Inn are engaged in a complex relationship and exchange that underscore epistemic oral structures and culturally determined practices of storytelling. Making clear the distinctions of class, literacy and comprehension between the travelers and the sophisticated narrator, the travelers' way of addressing one another effectively highlights the attributes that constitute an oral epistemic system and weaves them into the intricacy of the sophisticated narrator's literate engagement. Making possible a delicate equilibrium between the two systems, is one traveler whom the others respectfully call "worthy *Comis Ioniță*,"[22] a marginally educated freeman, whom the unnamed narrator of the *Tales* cleverly uses to facilitate interactions at the inn and to familiarize not only the highly literate narrator but also the readers with the cultural idiosyncrasies of the community of travelers. When news of a modern, Western Europe, are brought to Ancuța's Inn by agents of change like the Merchant Cristişor Dămian, the Comis acts as mediator and interpreter of the Merchant's travels as far away as Leipzig. In the ensuing dialogue that challenges their embedded cultural notions, the travelers hear about trains described as "a row of little houses on wheels fit on to iron rails […] drawn by a machine that whistles and puffs amazingly [and that] goes all by itself by means of fire, without horses," and deplore the lack in the West of specific Romanian culinary delights like "devilled lamb in garlic paste, sarmale, sour soup, or grilled carp," while marveling at the thought of "houses with four or five stories heaped on top of each other" and "streets made of one single piece of stone," and grumbling that sending girls to school is "another custom that they [the West] should keep to themselves" (98).

Illustrating what appears to be in *The Hatchet* yet another aspect of collective social memory, the spectacular wedding and funeral that Vitoria and her son encounter in their journey underscore the specific burdens orality places on cultural memory. Acting as a tenacious and reliable force in maintaining the apparatus of any civilization, these orally transmitted rituals lift Sadoveanu's storytelling to stimulating reflections on the vagaries of life that undercut the orally inflected expectation of mere social restoration and bring in the literate expectancy of a conventional novel. While conveying fidelity to human experience, the *Tales* develops an autonomously imaginative dimension – a narrative point of view that moves beyond the memory storage formulas of orality to communicate the novel's highly literate independence of vision and Sadoveanu's own personalization of village community.

And yet it seems precisely that these communities who can afford to narratively abandon the story of their communal self may also nurture individual characters whose existential dimensions become the means by which an orally inflicted narrative reaches autonomously imaginative exigencies. In the worlds of *The Hatchet* and the *Tales*, both Vitoria and Ancuţa bring into the narrative a transformative psyche, a vital reinforcement by which their characters' self-perpetuity is assured. And while this opening of the psyche to the outside world is no way meant to disparage oral storytelling (whose collective self is similarly outwardly oriented), it underscores the specific innovation required of a literate bias disengaged from the voice of orality and oriented toward the reared-on-literacy reader.

On a superficial narrative level, the self of both Vitoria and Ancuţa is fundamentally experienced in and through direct connection with others – the village world and the crowd of travelers at the inn. Once extricated from this community with which they identify for group definition, the two characters can begin to act for reasons that are no longer motivated by other persons or external circumstances. They become free, in a sense, to dwell on their existence as independent entities. While this process forces some kind of character isolation that may be anathema to the orally inflicted individual (i.e., the illiterate travelers at the inn, the village peasants Vitoria encounters), it also allows for the continued transformation of both Vitoria and Ancuţa and for the outgrowth, through their characters' development and resourcefulness, of a literally inflected narrative.

In *The Hatchet*, Vitoria's separation from the group fosters an increased and even articulable introspectivity, encouraging the character's private thought and enabling her to objectify her experiences. Given the narrative capacity for Vitoria's existential independence, she begins to exhibit character development and further detachment from the group as *The Hatchet* gradually subordinates the *Mioriţa* ballad to Vitoria's personal narrative, re-inscribing it in the space of modern Romania. In this context, Vitoria Lipan increasingly becomes the instrument for fashioning a "modern" Romanian woman. Unlike the absent feminine character in *Miorița*, the shepherd's mother who presumably accepts her son's death unconditionally, Vitoria Lipan disregards ancestral constraints and defies all odds as she goes boldly in her search for the murderers of her husband. Her journey takes her far away from her village and her encounters with various people all along the way sharpen her physical endurance and creative intelligence with highlighting her womanhood as part of the natural order of things.

In addition to the obvious differences in the development of the plot, far from being a mere re-telling of the *Miorița* ballad, *The Hatchet*'s fast-paced drama is a significant revision of traditional representations and resonates with the feminist model of relating femininity to authority. Having lost her husband, Vitoria can now partake of the kindness and friendship of the new people she encounters, and she seems to be as well-liked by strangers as he once was, exchanging her traditional femininity for a rewarding camaraderie that will then enable her to denounce her husband's murderers – not as a wronged woman, but as an individual voice assimilated within the community. Thus *The Hatchet*'s fictional world signals the story's departure from self-possessive feminism and simply celebrates Vitoria Lipan as someone who transcends patriarchal history and obtains complete self-emancipation to hold to justice two murderers responsible for the social disruption that the slaying of a friendly and generous man brings to the community.

In the traditional culture of Romania, a country divided for many centuries during its long and turbulent history, the community is never an abstract concept, but a concrete, social framework sustained by specific human relations between husband and wife, parent and child, older brother and younger brother, and, above all, one friend and another. Such a formulation defines an individual as a relational being and positions him or her in reciprocal obligations to others in the family, the clan, and the society. If the *Miorița* gives its readers a clear sense of the folk ballad's evolution into an instrument for ideological struggles, a process in which the ballad was constantly rewritten in versions that serve specific political premises, *The Hatchet* regulates the behavior of individual persons by requiring virtues that helped maintain the stability, as well as the harmony, of social relations. Although asserting as central the cardinal virtue of marital fidelity and moral integrity, *The Hatchet* also brings into relief Vitoria's quest for and public denunciation of her husband's murderers in order to restore both social order and rule of justice. Her actions, loyalty to the memory of her husband, and determination to find justice help maintain the continuity of a set of social relations that begins in the family and ends in the absolute authority of the community (which regards the family as its foundational unit).

In the final analysis Sodoveanu's recreation of the *Mioriţa* ballad in *The Hatchet* involves two narratives: Vitoria's personal narrative that openly celebrates her strength and wisdom by degendering the *Mioriţa* ballad to assert that women are often stronger than men, and a national narrative designed to place Vitoria's story in a specific social context delineated in full harmony with the enactment of folk traditions generally confined to an orally inflected narrative. As the story line develops, Vitoria's personal narrative is gradually subordinated to the national narrative, and the individual heroine increasingly becomes the instrument for fashioning a new woman, one capable of protecting and controlling her own life and family.

This formula of steering a narrative away from its generally collective, orally inflected orientation toward a mythical and literately inflicted character is repeated in the *Tales*, where the beautiful innkeeper Ancuţa is drawn into the narrative as a rich, resourceful female character of the type that function in Romanian folklore as mythic archetypes. If the inn is a picture of the relationship between men and women in the Moldavian community of the time where men dominate and rule over the public space as they drink wine and tell their stories, women like Ancuţa have their revenge. Nobody really cares about the inn's architecture, and most people who stop at the inn don't even notice its shape which men have erected. It is inside the inn where Ancuţa, like her mother before her, pours the wine, "stirs the fire smouldering under the ashes" (48) and presides over a place where reality and fantasy mix and where fine food, good wine, and good cheer welcome the travelers. The inn is thus Ancuţa's temple where she cooks and cleans, and where she has her role to play: connected to the cycle of the week, watching over its basic anthropological rhythms that include feeding, she makes livable and enjoyable the interior realm, the inside space which is warm, sheltering and comfortable. Like the archetypal figure of Sf. Vineri (Saint Friday) in Romanian folk tales, she is a mother figure, at home in a female universe of birth, germination and crops.

But she really can be much more than that. The story *The Other Ancuţa*, which is the fifth and central narrative among the total number of nine stories, introduces the other Ancuţa, the younger innkeeper's mother, as a woman-subject within the story itself. As a paragon of womanhood, prodigal in her gifts, and relentless in applying corrections, she dramatizes the inexhaustibility of female folk types that mediate between reality and imagination, human nature and supernatural creations. In an unjust feudal society, she devises a clever escape for the bold haiduk Todiriţă Cătană and his love, Lady Varvara, and her symbolic status becomes consonant with a modern woman-centered reinterpretation of Romanian culture. In helping the two lovers, who come from antagonistic social classes, the other Ancuţa uses her intellectual prowess to manipulate a patriarchal structure and to attain societal change through social *dis*-integration: with the two lovers' escape and subsequent marriage, love turns into a powerful weapon, a place of passage or a threshold where nature confronts a rigidly categorizing culture. A site for the transformation of the social power relations, the space of the inn where Todiriţă Cătană seeks shelter becomes a ferociously feminine place. Here the other Ancuţa humbles the power structure and reinscribes the traditional roles of men and women in a space that eschews stillness and silence.

If expression in the oral culture is fundamentally tied to the voice, the inn is the visual site or the space of oral rhetoric. Experienced primarily as utterance, the stories told at the inn provide a narrative example that is heavily orally inflected and thus devoid of immediate cultural aplomb. The absence of locale, the whatness of a place like Ancuţa's Inn, leads to the unassimilated moments of visions disconnected from our cultural appropriation and memory. To be assimilated, such visions require the enabling dimension of literacy that is essential to take orality out of the ordinary and transform mere site into place. As if to explain the need for a detailed set and décor for the *Tales*, Sadoveanu, in a short note that precedes 1964 edition of the novel, raises the issue of the inn's authenticity. Bringing his own childhood memories into the discussion, Sadoveanu declares that his own mother had spent her childhood in the region around the inn "in a poor little village called Verşeni," and that he himself had seen it as a child whenever he went to visit his grandparents. Sadoveanu proclaims categorically that Ancuţa's Inn is no fiction. It actually existed and was famous in the past century. Its ruined walls still stood some ten years ago when the last heirs divided the bricks to build two modest farm houses for themselves, not very distant from each other" (17).

By turning orality into literacy Sadoveanu's own reportage becomes the very basis of the narrative and visual texture – the very impulse by which memory is articulated to legitimize narration. From the start, the narrator states that the inn is rigid and symmetrical, muscular and protected with barred gates which look like an armor:

> Ancuţa's Inn was not merely an inn, but a genuine fortress. It had walls as thick as from here to way over there, and barred gates such as I've never seen in my life. People, cattle, and carts could take shelter within and be without fear of the thieves and robbers.
>
> At the time I'm speaking of there was still peace in the land and good will amongst men. The gates of the inn stood wide open like those at the

> Prince's court. And on mild autumn days you could see the Moldova Valley through them, stretching as far as the eye could see, and the mountain mists on the evergreen forests as far away as Ceahlău and Hălăuca. And, when the sun buried itself in the other world and the distant landscape dimmed and slid into dark mystery, the fires in the courtyard lighted up the stone walls, the dark recesses of the doors and the latticed windows. (20)

The combination of the geometry, the phallic imagery, and the way in which the building looks like a man in armor, an intimidating gate and outside geometry of stone walls with the high gates that send out travelers across the Moldavian land, are inextricably tied to the ability to depart from the mere visual and the human voice. Demanding a literate inventiveness, the description of the inn reflects a different sort of reality, one that accords reality the opportunity to be constructed beyond and above the voice, in a quieter way, deviating from the oral episteme, through the inflections of a literacy intellectually comprehensible and performatively engaging.

As monographs of village culture in which oral articulations give way to the spectatorial quietude of what Roland Barthes calls writerly (scriptable) literature,[23] *The Hatchet* and *Tales* offer a canonization of folklore, a rewriting of ancestral and archetypal myths, and a refinement of oral poetry and storytelling that are collected, recycled, concentrated and artistically rendered to subvert any possibility of dichotomizing orality and literacy and to preclude any supposition that orality is merely a holdover voice from more primitive days.

CHAPTER 5

Experiencing the Past, Narrating the Present: Magical Realism as Narrative Discourse in Ştefan Agopian's *Velvet Tache*

> If you are to venture to interpret the past you can do so only out of the fullest exertions of the vigours of the present...
>
> Nietzsche, *Untimely Meditations*

> The Man whom we can with justice call 'modern' is solitary. He is also of necessity and at all times, for every step towards a fuller consciousness of the present removes him further from his original participation mystique with the mass of men – from submission in a common consciousness.
>
> Seymour Menton, *Magic Realism Rediscovered 1918-1981*

In none of its applications to Romanian literature has the concept of Magical Realism ever successfully differentiated between itself and "established" genre systems such as Realism and Romance. Thus, it is not surprising that critics have abandoned the term altogether, in spite of its startling development in recent years. My purpose in this preface is to employ a little of the liberty provided by Romanian Magical Realism's lack of theoretical specificity and, rather than attempt to define the concept in terms of its genre, to place it within the context of literary and cultural hybridity by taking a close look at Ştefan Agopian's novel of 1981, *Velvet Tache*.[1]

The novel takes as its focal point the tumultuous first half of the nineteenth century in Romania. Stylistically Agopian's narrative is generally regarded as a stepping stone in the emancipation of Romanian fiction from the dogmatic Socialist Realism of the 1950s, and the attempts at the canonical Realism of the 1970s and 1980s of Romanian prose.[2] What still remains to be addressed in discussing *Velvet Tache* are the specific elements of the novel as both historical narrative, and magical realist text that also involves strange and supernatural free play and fantasy, and that refutes categorically the imperatives of Socialist Realism.

Emerging from meditative processes, *Velvet Tache* offers a new type of metanarrative marked by the manipulation of time and space relations and stretching as far as Romanian folklore and myth to create the illusion of a narrative articulated by an individual's experience that is both timeless and historical. Associated with Magical Realism, this writing of history based on individual experience not only makes it possible for us to understand an entire community of people at a particular time in Romania's history, but it also functions as an empowering narrative solution by which the author uses the past to write about the present. Far from being disconnected from reality, the bleak picture of the moral indifference and psychological isolation, along with other social ills that have been pervaded the first half of nineteenth-century Romania chronicled in *Velvet Tache* echo Agopian's own time (the 1980s Romania as a decade marked by police terror, fear, and the aberrant communist ideology of Nicolae Ceausescu's totalitarian regime).

Effected in subtle and indirect ways, the novel's connection to the present stresses Agopian's use of magical elements to suggest not only that repetition of violent and destructive patterns in history may by cyclical and inescapable, but also to imply that our reality – in part the result of human character and in part conditioned by societal and cultural values – is more complex than we know, a comforting notion during times of political oppression.

To ascertain the extent to which Agopian abandons traditional Realism to generate a novel disguised as a historical document and uses Magical Realism as a means to radically modify and replenish traditional realism, I rely on recent scholarship that has received much attention in the last several decades and is particularly relevant to the case of *Velvet Tache*.[3] One way to start when addressing the issue of Magical Realism as a literary practice operative in Agopian's novel is to consider Robert Kroetsch's and Linda Kenyon's observation that Magical Realism seems to be closely linked with "living on the margins" from imperial centers and their totalizing systems of generic classification.[4] Located on the geographic borderlines of European culture, at the eastern extremity of Central Europe, Romanian culture has been simultaneously "on the margins" and under the spell of the centralizing impulse of Western cultures whose literary models it has systematically incorporated.[5] Specifically, *Velvet Tache* foregrounds a magical realist narrative that borrows from and relies on major literary structures typical of Western cultures while at the same time offering a historical narrative rooted in the indigenous Romanian culture in which it is set.[6]

In this context, of particular interest for my discussion of Agopian's text as a superimposition of literary and indigenous narrative traditions, as well as a powerfully appealing hybrid of the realist and the fantastic, are (1) Michael Valdez Moses's claim that Magical Realism is a fusion of two distinct narrative traditions that establishes the paternity of the magical realist novel to the Western European realist novel of the eighteenth and nineteenth centuries, and its maternity to a different and distinct reservoir of native-to-the-region or pre-modern materials;[7] and (2) José Monleén's view that such archaic materials specific to a region are in turn rooted in the cultural and historical contexts, and complete with their penchant for fabulation, metafiction, the fantastic, or the marvelous.[8]

Told as a retrospective and unlikely projection from beyond the protagonist's grave, but filled with concrete, historical details provided by a first-person narrator befitting a realistic novel, *Velvet Tache* examines the time of Tache Vlădescu's life, as well as that of his ancestors and of everyone who has ever figured in his life. In a remarkable assemblage of revelatory details about rural communities observed in various aspects of their life - hunting, sexual practices, village rituals – the novel becomes a chronicle of the historical, social, and political scene of the first half of the nineteenth-century province of Oltenia in southwestern Romania, beginning with Tache's birth in 1800 and ending with his death in 1848. Grafted into the historiographic metafiction are significant historical events, such as the Turks' 1812-14 frequent incursions north of the Danube into Oltenia at a time when Gavrilă Vlădescu, the landowner (or *boyar*) of the Mălura estate and Tache's own father, is murdered by the Turks who set fire to his leader Tudor Vladimirescu whose army the adolescent Tache and his close friends, Boyar Lăpai and the Dwarf, plan to join; and the faint echoes of the Eteria, and 1848 Revolution circulating around the time when Tache is to be murdered by his step-brother, Mamona the Young, whose yearning to take over the Vlădescu manor and estate was triggered on the very first day when his father, Mamona the Old, married Tache's mother after defeating the other contenders for her hand. Tache's retrospective retelling, whose narrative structure closely resembles a Romanian "chronicle of a death foretold," ends with Tache's forthcoming death on the eve of his son's birth, a death that would leave not only the Vlădescus estate, but also his new wife, Flora, at the center of the dreaded encounter with Mamona the Young.

Stretching imaginative possibilities to energize a release of Romania's troubled history, *Velvet Tache* pushes us backward, toward the past, through narrative accounts like the one recounting Tache's father's breeding of ferocious German dogs for the purpose of attacking the Turks who regularly pillaged his estate:

> Father liked the idea and, as soon as he recovered, purchased three pairs of the kind they call "bear biters." To these he added several other pairs of dogs, as large as calves, called *mollosses*. Now he was busy with breeding them and looking after the puppies, and he forgot about us altogether. The dogs proved fierce, which made Father very happy. When they almost killed a beggar, Father got drunk with joy. The

> peasants didn't have the courage to cross the estate by themselves anymore after this incident. After giving it much thought, Father decided he didn't have enough dogs yet, so he bought ten more shepherd dogs of the Komodor breed. These were steppe dogs, and, in spite of their lovely aspect, they soon proved to be genuine beasts by nature. To make them even more savage, he would let them starve and then flog them. Then he let them loose at night, and the gang proved more dangerous than a pack of wolves. Whenever Mother got a chance to catch him in a moment of leisure, she tried to talk to him and even scold him, but it was in vain. Father only had eyes for his dogs. Because of them, our servants began to run away. Father managed to capture one and, gathering the rest of the servants to witness it, he gave the unfortunate man to the starved dogs for a prey. He didn't let them kill the guy, but he became an epileptic from the fear he endured and died a month later. (77-8)

In his treatment of events governed by such unspeakable violence, Agopian renders the occurrences of 1980s Romania in symbolic historical narrative. While exaggerating the lack of logic and common sense of Gavrilă Vlădescu's behavior, these aberrant actions simultaneously offer an oblique commentary on the moral dissolution disturbing moral indifference, and psychological isolation of contemporary Romania's political leaders projected indirectly through the many horrible, violent events in the country's past.

Throughout a narrative whose time is neither linear or predictable, Tache's memory consecrates the authority of his own deeds and words over the laws of nature and the principles of logic, and even over his own death, as it unleashes the narrative events that rely heavily on the motifs of Romance listed by Northrop Frye:[9] the mysterious births and lives of Tache's ancestors in obscure times in history, prophecies about the future contortions of the plot that pose a challenge to realist conventions of uniform space and time and verisimilitude, adventures that induce in the reader a sense of unreality, such as the marriages of both Tache and of his father to women about whom nothing is certain, not even their real names or parentage. But although Tache's story has the shape of a traditional romance, it engages the readers only as a parody of the genre. Unlike the demure and innocent maiden of a romance, Flora Fruscio, Tache's future wife, travels in the caravan of itinerant actors and seduces the narrator one night at a country inn. In similar ways, Tache's mother, Zamfira Lupu, forces Tache's father to marry her so as to stop her screaming about what she claims is old Gavrilă Vlădescu's theft and appropriation of her dead father's body to study the cholera epidemic and its effects on its victims. Finally, unlike the hero of a romance, Tache never takes himself seriously and, beyond the extraordinary method of writing from beyond the grave, his narrative is not a grand rendition of a splendid life. It is instead an account in which the narrator turned Author, standing totally apart from his narrated life, elbows his readers from the very beginning, questioning, lecturing, and challenging to them to make their own sense of his irreverent and chatty ramblings and of his unheroic life:

> And now I do nothing but lie here six feet under, and slowly rot in eternity, thinking and speaking, and knowing my words and thoughts belong to somebody else (the one who, with your permission – for I have to give him a name – we shall call "Author"). I could give him another name, but as there is no special honor, or difference in a name, I will call him by this convention. (39)

Unmasking romantic conventions and ridiculing artistic strategies by revealing the mechanisms used by traditional writers in the construction of their plots and narratives, the novel's opening section and wildly inventive story line project an eminently satirical narrative that displays reality in a fragmented and tattered state, forcing the reader to fill in the voids. By this reading, Tache's narrative is both a terrible, strange, and mystical story hiding the unreal in the shards of the broken glass of reality. It is also a typically Romanian trickster story, complete with parodic twists and seriocomic characters that the narrator continually and hilariously mocks. Tache's friends are recognizable as both stock characters of Romanian folklore and humorous distortions of Western models. We have, for instance, the socially inept second-tier Boyar Lăpai and his brother, the ingenious and rambunctious Dwarf. As Eugen Negrici points out,[10] the presence of Boyar Lăpai as a humorous Tăndală – sleepy and awkward, while being simultaneously shrewd, and of the Dwarf, reduced to the size of a diminutive Achilles in proportional armor – touch on a special kind of Balkanic fabulation, complete with types specific to Romanian folklore's variety of the uncanny and the marvelous, and the comic distortion of a well known Western model. That is, the odd pairing initiates a kind of double vision into a marginal culture, a binary dimension within the novel's narrative achieved by transporting a Romanian cultural type like the beloved Tăndală to a twentieth-century perspective, as well as by simultaneously imposing a western heroic type in the comically altered version of a Western court-jester-Dwarf on the indigenous space of a Romanian province.

Moving between reality and legend or history and myth, *Velvet Tache* does not enforce a clear separation between the two and defines itself in as complete a manner as possible through a recourse to both.

Fitting nicely into Angel Flores's expanded definition of Magical Realism, Agopian's novel is an "amalgamation of realism and fantasy" that achieves "a transformation of the common and everyday into the awesome and the unreal" and where "time exists in a kind of timeless fluidity and the unreal happens as part of reality." Even though readers are able to identify the specific historical time in which *Velvet Tache*'s narrative takes place, the novel's characters exist in their own isolated microcosms that are not explicitly connected to a familiar world. Simultaneously, however, in keeping with Luis Leal's concept of *lo realismo maravilloso, Velvet Tache* also deals with objective reality and attempts to discover the mystery that exists in objects, life, and human actions, without resorting to fantastic elements.[11]

As a mythical and historical space, Oltenia is an *imago mundi*, located at the center of the world and providing for the continuity and participation of its people as a symbolic transmigration that allows escape into other periods and accommodates the need to live in multiple eras at the same time. In spite of a certain narrative uncertainty and vagueness of the events, both Gavrilă Vlădescu and Tache himself are good Christians who accept their Mălura estate as uncharted territory, a place where the present history of redemption is made, either in the form of a deadly fight of Eastern Orthodoxy against the Ottoman Turks[12] or in the confrontation with the forces of evil personified by Mamona the Young. Frequently used by Romanian historians, this stylistic device known as *heterochrony*[13] allows for the overlap of several temporal sequences and further enriches Agopian's narrative discourse with an amplification of the scale and categories of reality. Thus, it enables Tache to avoid living fully or for extended periods in his own time and space and to see the present as being organically connected to ages past, which are imitated and restored by Tache's own actions and deeds. Concomitantly, the exaggerated horrors of reality in Tache's story, such as the brutal and unlawful imprisonment of Mamona the Old, who is left to starve in a cell-like room, and the greed and ruthfulness of Mamona the Young, who wishes to appropriate the Mălura estate for his own benefit and who betrays revolutionary ideals and his comrades' trust, seem to mirror the unsettling aspects of communism as they allow Agopian to incorporate Romania's political and social realities in the text without being openly political.

Finally, *heterochrony* introduces one of the basic traits of Romanian collective consciousness: a recurrence of the archetypes of death and rebirth and of cyclical experiences passed on from one generation to the next that not only tend toward a more effective participation of the symbols and myths, but also suggest that no social order, no matter how oppressive, is either permanent or infallible; and that it is possible and, in fact, necessary to bear all hardships by adopt-ting various strategies of escapism, such as immersion in compensatory historical fiction.

Infringing upon the natural and human realities of time and place, while simultaneously relying on verifiable historical circumstances and events, *Velvet Tache* proposes an unexpected richness of romanticized storytelling in such improbable juxtapositions and marvelous mixtures as Tache's father's chance encounter at a country inn with Zamfira Lupu, the woman who will become Tache's mother, and Tache's own meeting with his future wife, Flora, in similar circumstances and with the same outcome, almost half a century later; or the superimposition of Tache's childhood alliance with Boyar Lăpai and the Dwarf to stave off the killing of Mamona the Old at the hands of his own son, Mamona the Young, over adult Tache's attempt to fight the same killer, who is out to get him at the time of the narrative present.

Further appropriating Western structures, *Velvet Tache* relies on the three dimensions characteristic of a realistic *Bildungsroman*: marriage, death, and the transmutation of life into art. As in most works belonging to this genre, such as the novels of Charles Dickens, Stendhal, or Balzac, the perspectives of Tache, as the child who begins to experience the world and as the adult master of Mălura who remembers those experiences, correspond to the novel's two different but adjacent narratives. Like Dickens's protagonist Pip, a young man who places himself at the centre of a story of great expectations and lost illusions, Tache projects a double narrative of himself as a child who is the hero of great escapes and extraordinary deeds, like those he spends in old Isaac Herţog's medicine shop, and as the adult narrator, the gloomy master of the Mălura estate, who has surrendered cherished ideals and now comes to regard life as a hard and unforgiving lesson. Thus Tache's withdrawal from day-to-day life and the refuge he finds in books and famous quotes, as well as his purely intellectual responses to Plato's *Republic*, reflect his understanding of the world around him and ultimately his appreciation of the comfort great works can bring to the gruesome quality of life. Such engagement with real-life experiences and appreciation of books infuse Tache's narrative with an authority that seems an outgrowth of the convergence of the popular and intellectual cultures of his time and therefore validates Tache's comments and implicit criticism of the events that he witnesses.

This awareness and ability allows Tache to detach himself, transcribe his life, and present his writings as his memoirs. From this angle, unlike Pip and most heroes of the realist *Bildungsroman*, who place themselves at the center of a narrative of lost illusions and expectations, and *not* the falseness of those ideals and expectations. Although he may be considered a cynic or even a radical skeptic, Tache seems to embrace a form of deceptive realism, a kind of realism that allegorically describes, in a somewhat devious and disguised way, the social circumstances of nineteenth-century Oltenia as metonymic of Romania's historical past and as a space that transcends the limitations of a chronologically specific context. It seems as though Tache's memoirs and his bitter disappointments, which show his essential link to the nation and its history, are not only a trip back in time but also connect with Agopian's readers – first to the extent that all stories, and their meanings, always reflect in various degrees of transparency the times of their author's life; and second, through that sort of process by which the readers of Tache's memoirs, by participating in the narrative discourse, enter the record of history. The outcome of this engagement is an alchemical process by which Tache's dissatisfaction with his times triggers a transparent analogy with the current circumstances of Agopian's contemporaries, who may have felt the same clash between their social expectations and the abject practices of Ceaunescu's brand of communism, the time of monstrous physical and emotional demolition they had to endure in 1980s Romania.[14]

From beyond his grave, Tache ostensibly writes his memoirs to expose and emphasize his ordinary status with a frankness that only a dead man can have, in a narrative that occasionally resembles Tache's drunken ramble. This immediate narrative level, however, also entails a subversive strategy that is anything but straightforward and by which events from the past are oblique comments on not-so-remote historical occurrences and simultaneously validate Tache's point of view as a likely commentary on contemporary issues. Here one must note the childhood episode when Tache, abandoned by his mother, a woman who seriously undermines the sanctification of maternal devotion as the role most gratifying to women in Romanian culture, hides himself in the old chest kept in a dark corner of Isaac Herţog's medicine shop. The events Tache witnesses, such as the torture and murder of the town's Jews (foreshadowing, in the early 1800s, subsequent atrocities committed against Central and Eastern European Jewry) and his emergence from the chest where he had been hiding as if in a second womb when the attack ends, mark a metaphorical second birth that confers upon Tache a special orphan status, and singular characteristics.

As a local version of an Ishmael adrift in the world, Tache can speak out forcefully and ground himself in the existing realities of one time or another. Even though this anchoring in actuality is periodically dislodged, particularly during those times when Tache, reinforcing a kinship not of blood but of orphanhood, joins Boyar Lăpai and the Dwarf to confront and fight against the evil alliance of Mamona the Young and the sinister Vaucher, Tache's French tutor who replaces Old Mamona in Tache's mother's bed, nothing like a complete rhetoric of fantasy takes place. Rather, and aura of unknowability and mystery, coupled with a theme of unpredictability and lack of control over events transfuses the narrative providing new ways of transcending the oppressive reality with "a sustained opposition … to an established system of realist representation."[15]

Throughout the novel these two contrasting views of the world are presented as if to forestall the possibility of interpretive closure through an act of naturalizing the text to an established system of dual representation by means of Tache himself who, as the self-proclaimed Author and narrator of his memoirs, has two voices. Sometimes he depicts events from a rational point of view, and sometimes from that of a believer in magic who resorts to myths and Romanian ethnocultural beliefs without seeing any inconsistency, but presenting all events instead as two sides of the same coin that are not mutually exclusive. In this context, a more appropriate theoretical approach to Agopian's narrative would be to examine Tache's perspective through the three different types of Magical Realism that William Spindler[16] categorizes as metaphysical, anthropological, and ontological, with the understanding that there are many points of overlap between them and that they are interchangeable and by no means mutually exclusive.

The first type, metaphysical, corresponds to the original definition of Magical Realism and is used to describe familiar scenes as if they were something new and unknown, but without dealing especially with the supernatural. Such scenes that seem "recognizable as within the boundaries of the real" (Spindler 80) and yet induce a sense of unreality in the readers, feature a variety of settings: ordinary country inns as sites for outlandish occurrences (of the type that brings the corpse of a cholera victim to Gavrila Vladescu's room at his own request) or grotesque encounters (like the surreal brawl between the Dwarf and the fat whorish woman who bites his leg mortally); rooms with bolted doors and windows that bear only superficial similarities with those of the real world, like the place where Old Mamona, immured and reading Diogenes while sunflowers grow between his toes, awaits his death at the hands of his murderers, his own son, Mamona the Young, and Vaucher, the French tutor who ends up marrying Tache's mother (175-76); or alien and disconcerting places, used as spaces almost within grasp and yet unknown, like the living room and summer pavilion of the Vlădescus's manor where Tache's mother, tired of being a widow, receives her unlikely suitors on April 19, 1812. Although the time and geography of this particular event are all-too-real, the uncanny atmosphere of the courtship – which ends with Tache's mother fainting and being carried away to the pavilion in the arms of Old Mamona – produces on the readers an eerie, both serene and melancholy, effect that legitimizes the child Tache's feelings of helplessness and confusion.

Adding to the preternatural surroundings, the suitors' depiction in a De Chirico *Pittura metafisica* style that Spindler associates with metaphysical Magical Realism confers on them an impersonal and static quality and an illusion of surreal uniqueness.
With their disturbing, toy-like appearance, the second-tier Boyar Lăpai "riding around our house on a skinny shell of a horse ... sitting like a pole thrust into the rump of the beast (as if someone thrust a pole into the side of a beast you could somehow call a horse only due to the harness, that is the saddle, the reins, and the rest of straps and buckles; and on the back of this animal, sat a pole with a little beard at its end) [173]", the filthy rich Greek merchant like "a mountain of flesh, bones, and fat – a gigantic, inhuman ball (187)"; and the attorney Gingă emerging as "a funny little man ... dressed up in an evening suit and an enormous silk hat on his head ... hopping about and swirling around the cane he was holding in his hand like a sword (189-90)" trigger in the young Tache an unsettling effect of both humorous and monstrous unreality and convey to the entire scene an aura of mystery that is achieved without resorting to the supernatural.

The next category, the anthropological magical realism in which the narrator usually has "two voices," proposes a presentation of events from both a rational and a magical point of view. This type of narrative juxtaposition allows Tache to tap on the myths, folklore, and cultural background that form the collective consciousness of the Romanian people. Moving beyond a realist representation, the black dog impersonating the devil and the evil person of Ladorică Săulescu, the faithful servant of Mamona the Young who accompanies Tache on his surreal journey to the Draga Monastery, brings into Tache's story spectral apparitions and unearthly ghouls that reflect and validate popular superstitions by which the devil is said to lure men into eternal damnation unless they are vigilant in their faith:

> A large dog turned up from somewhere, watching us with mad eyes. The sun was darkened by the large back of our cart driver, Părvu, who, up on his feet, was whipping the horses. Drowned in fog, Părvu seemed to be floating like a threat above us.
> "What's the matter, Părvu?" I asked.
> And suddenly the laughter of Lădorica Săulescu rose above the ravines.
> "The dog over there," Părvu replied, and Lădorica's laughter again covered us like water.
> "Why did you get scared, Master?" Lădorica asked, and gave another laugh, distorting his face until it turned into Lădorica the hound that was pursuing us. And the dog turned into Lădorica, running after us and laughing. When everything was over, Lădorica said with a merry voice:

> "The devil is close by."
> "The gracious Lord has put us to the test," Părvu said, and he pulled the reins, slowing down the steaming horses. (58)

Beyond the preoccupation with uncanny elements that link the novel's anthropological Magical Realism to superstitions and popular culture, Tache's narrative depicts characters that possess a magical consciousness or seem controlled by occult principles. Both the former barber Şopârlă, later known as the holy monk Silent Gregory, and the gifted Dwarf, who can piece together in astonishing ways all the characters' past actions and thoughts as if he had witnessed them, are depicted as extraordinary creatures; more importantly, their prodigious deeds and accomplishments, such as the holy monk's healing powers and miracles, and the Dwarf's numerous inventions, like the solar clock with lenses from Amsterdam pulled by the ten gypsies, are regarded by the narrator-turned-Author as equal, if not superior, to Western science and technology.

Further evidence of *Velvet Tache*'s anthropological Magical Realism is reflected in a preoccupation with the grotesque, deformity, and exaggeration – particularly in the characters' appearance. Chief among them is the unforgettable description of Louis André Gabriel Bombast Vaucher, Tache's tutor, whose exaggerated horror marks the dissolution of the character's human identity:

> A little bent, his eyes staring into the void, Vaucher had long and thin hands resembling some dusty sunflower stems, two of them, and at the end of those stems, there were other sticks, five plus five, like some glass tubes, with nails, and flesh and bones, and on them, as if what you'd seen that wasn't enough, a lot of rings of tin and copper and silver, brushed and a little oxidized in black and red and green and milky white, moldy and poisonous oxides pleasant to the ignorant eye. Between the sticks of his arms, vaguely holding on to them, there was the body of a huge cockroach, a *blatta orientalis*, as the Dwarf was going to say sometimes, looking at him just how I used to, and on that body there hung clothes and trinkets and a watch from which you could only see the chain and the little wheel you turn when it stops. From that body emerged a thin and long neck like a starved transparent intestine, in which the voice was implanted, and beside the voice, the rattle of a monotonous breathing, as well as the needs of the coughing and sneezing and swallowing and hiccupping. At the end of the neck, like a sort of swelling, some unfinished cancer that made you feel sick, there was a ball on which you could see first a

> long and thin nose resembling a hairy leaf rippling in the November wind of dying year. On one side and the other, there were the eyes, resembling two caterpillars which have the ambition to blink from time to time, and by their blinking, release a pasty white-gray look, as if you'd stepped on them in search of this, and after stepping, see what would come out of their thin membrane, that amorphous and dull substance, like a greenish and gray and slippery sort of clay. And up there on this ball, you could see a worn-out silk hat, and in this silk hat, a tiny hole on either side, letting a feeble light pass through, as if its master had been shot some time in the silk hat. And from under this hat, behind the eyes, protruding rarely, but substantially, the strands of hair, resting long and shiny on a collar as tall as possible and as greasy; as if one hundred spiders had descended in time from a silk hat down a collar. And on those hairs, like some little boats, dandruff shining like mother-of-pearl; and on the collar, a graveyard of little boats rotting lazily. (236-37)

As an updated version of a character out of old horror tales, Vaucher's Portrait seems intended both to horrify the readers and to force them to accept the intrusion of the monstrous into the real world where it corrupts any noble thought and destroys desire. In Tache's story, Vaucher's grotesque coupling with Tache's mother leads to a sequence of tragedies that culminate in the deaths of both Mamona the Old and Tache's mother.

Finally, the ontological Magical Realism of *Velvet Tache* presents the supernatural in a matter-of-fact way, as if it did not contradict reason, and offers no explanations for the unreal events in the text and no recourse to any particular cultural perspective. Tache does not appear to be puzzled when he brings in and out of the story as if it were a normal part of ordinary everyday life an assorted number of devils and angels who seem to be around at all times, intersecting the paths of the characters and intervening in their actions. The lazy evening, for instance, when "a tiny, bristling devil," enchanted with the evening music produced by pipes, "sneaked in happily between me and Boyar Lăpai, in the unbearable warmth of our ribs, and from there, like from a theater box, he listened to the tune with a happy and shining white grin on his face (316)", becomes for the boy Tache an essential part of a widely recognizable reality that includes the deliberately realistic setting of Mălura, or Boyar Lăpai's estates, and suggests neither the unusual nor the uncanny. Throughout the novel, the lack of antimony between the natural and the supernatural is underplayed by representing the supernatural almost accidentally, as in those narrative moments when Tache casually describes himself and his pregnant wife Flora floating around the rooms, or when he watches the Dwarf floating:

> Finally, one evening, immediately after midnight, I observed the ascension of the Dwarf in the air – sitting cross-legged and apparently sleeping with open, and glassy and cold eyes, with no expression in them at all, just floating in the air like a dead body; not minding a thing. (283)

Placing the ordinary and the extraordinary on the same level of reality, the Dwarf's self-portrait offers no apparent sense of mystery or suspense in the representation of "his dark green uniform of an Austrian army colonel before 1800, the color of a pine-tree in winter (275)." It is simply an invitation to accept the ontological reality of the canvas:

> Seated in front of an easel and a mirror, the Dwarf was painting his self-portrait. He had already drawn his moustaches and a colonel's epaulets while listening to me, then for several evenings running he painted on the rest of the canvas a deserted mill full of moulds and an angel resembling a crow contemplating the mill. Then he painted himself in the form of a devil with a hussar colonel's epaulets, somehow astride the angel about to take flight. He finished the painting fast enough when we had already decided in favor of painting, yet, not knowing when we were going to do it; taking one step back, he contemplated his work with satisfaction. (274)

Beyond and within these representations, the possibility of metamorphoses makes it possible for the narrative to be told from the perspective of a dead man, and for the presence of death to be less threatening and irreversible; the narrative takes the view that life and reality are only a collective construction, and ultimately point to a strong relationship between Magical Realism and a type of historical realism that ensures a necessary relationship with imagined history. This assertion, which is achieved when something very ordinary is presented as if it were a real prodigy by describing it through the eyes of a character (the child Tache) for whom this is the case, underscores the importance of realism in the overall structure of *Velvet Tache*. Brought to infuse the narrative with authority, the realist component of the novel allows for the possibility that Agopian's brushes with Magical Realism stress the complex interaction between the familiar, physical world and what lies beyond rational explanation, and thus transcribes both the historical past and, on a more subversive level, the country's more immediate political predicament.

There certainly is fictional reality in Tache's insistence on his genetic identity, by which he is the only righteous heir of the Mălura estate, and of his title guaranteed in a premodern Romanian society. But such insistence poses a challenge to Tache's other, social identity, by which Mamona the Young, Tache's step-brother, has equal rights to the estate. Underscoring this social identity is the novel's background that features well documented historical events, e.g., the failed 1821 Revolution led by Tudor Vladimirescu,[17] and the 1848 Revolution whose demogratic slogans and programmatic overthrow of inherited privilege are echoed fictionally in the restlessness of Tache's servants and in the country priest's ramblings.

As narrator of his own life, Tache is well aware of the arbitrariness of his inherited title, and finds, in principle, no reason for one to be rich and another poor. Indeed, he sees no good reason for doing anything about it, i.e., fighting against Mamona the Young. Such a violent fight would destabilize the estate even beyond the 1848 upheaval and contradict Tache's basic sense of social relativity by which his constructed narrative identity is not conservative. But neither is it progressive or radical, since Tache argues in favor of order and stability in the discussion with the local priest, who is himself an ally of the rebel faction.

Thus, although Tache, the master from Mălura, claims in the abstract that class differences based on the birthright are arbitrary, he clings to his identity as a function of the world that has made him by recommending himself from the start as one who "come[s] from a not-very-ancient family – but again not one of those that you can frequently see (40)." He whips his servants even without reason, acts as a man in charge whose orders are always to be obeyed, and thinks of the outlaws led by Mamona the Young as hooligans who need to be expelled from the world he inhabits, without understanding them as agents in a natural, historical process of erasing the old social order. In such respects, Tache's life resembles that of Faulkner's characters who are caught between the claustrophobic and stagnant atmosphere of rural communities and their own vivid imagination, and whose lives are subtly but consistently overshadowed by the past of their societies – the bygone era of slave-holding Yoknapatawpha in Faulkner's fiction and the serfs and gypsies of Oltenia's feudal order. With its half-forgotten but still powerful sway, such past affects Tache's life not only with strong infusions of magical and superstitious beliefs, but also in exercising a strong influence on his social mentality that refuses to allow for a different social order.

Although the same age, Tache and Mamona the Young seem to be generated by antagonistic social forces: with a *Weltanschaung* generated by magical and mythical beliefs that hold no stake in the modern state, Tache appears to be countering the forces of capitalist modernity that produce Mamona the Young. (Notably, the name Mamona is associated in Romanian culture with Satan, the Devil,[18] and also with avarice and greed, both attributes of an evil and sinful nature.) Supporting the likelihood that the two characters may be reflecting the move from a pre-modern to a modern Romanian state, their social status parallels a historical shift that Michel Foucalt traces from a discourse based on blood, specific to premodern collectives imagined in terms of connections based on inheritance, to one based on adversarial relations imagined as a struggle for power in modern society.

In these terms, Agopian's novel facilitates a transition from a story with limited, regional scope to the national epic space by which Tache's narrative illustrates a critical and complex transition from pre-modern to modern Romania. Turning history into tale, the novel foregrounds a historical narrative that carries the readers backward to capture a historical past, when the Mălura estate could be passed from father to son in the legitimate terms prescribed by lineage and ancestry. Simultaneously, the story depicts the infiltration of a new social order by which Mamona the Young, the violent social outlaw and dishonest rebel who plots and schemes to inherit the Mălura estate after murdering Tache and who steals the money ostensibly collected for revolutionary purposes, ultimately challenges genetic parentage and societal taboos to destroy the velvety social fabric of Tache's ancestors. All along, by addressing events that occurred in the past, the narrative reads back into events that occur concomitantly in the present of Romania's violent political regime.

Making sense of the phenomenal world through the novel's storytelling, Tache's Mălura estate functions as a premodern world, and Tache's character as simply standing for the old social order threatened by the evil forces of modernity. Viscerally inimical to the stable contexts in which people once lived, such forces impart anxiety and terror and are fictionally personified in the novel by Young Mamona: he is the revolutionary "new man," whose infamy and opportunism (not unlike the ideological masquerade and police terror of Romania's communist era) are turned into virtues that aim to destroy a traditional society and to completely reconstruct the displayed classes and social hierarchy into a different mold – a political matrix that Agopian's readers, removed by more than a century from Tache's world, could identify as the destructive hammer of 1980s Romania.

Such a narrative outcome that urges the shift of *Velvet Tache* into the political mode suggests in the novel's historical and political dimension embedded within a magical realist text. As it emerges in Tache's story, the dawn of a modern Romanian nation-state builds itself out of the ruins for the Mălura estate in the form of a melancholy metanarrative organized around the free play of Magical Realism and built on fragmented images of violence and destruction. While destabilizing realistic representation, Agopian's Magical Realism outstrips traditional narrative forms to include an ingenious reconsideration of Romania's historical past, myth and traditional belief and relies on an unseen world of cultural wholeness that articulates the unsaid to inscribe in Velvet Tache an extraordinary "historical" tale.[19]

Beyond this narrative complexity, however, and in the context of Agopian's contemporary political reality, the relationship between *Velvet Tache*'s Magical Realism and the reality of Romania's oppressive communist regime reaches a different form of distinction. In line with what some critics consider Magical Realism as compensatory fiction diverting them from political action,[20] *Velvet Tache* puts forward an alternative discourse that offers a curative and therapeutic narrative, a text that can be considered to perform, on an immediate level, a cultural function similar to that which Walter Scott's historical romances fulfilled in their day.[21] Specifically, the pre-modern confines of Tache's world represented in Agopian's magical realist novel possess a nostalgic appeal and sentimental attraction that allow the reader to reside temporarily within a virtual organic community without having to assume the social burdens and obligations of the contemporary social scene. Beyond this type of escapism, however, the romantic allure of *Velvet Tache*'s Magical Realist narrative makes it possible for readers not only to escape both to and from what Salmon Rushdie calls "an imaginary homeland," but also to respond to the harshness of communist Romania through a text that provides an alternative history – one that proposes compensatory narrative engagement to heal the trauma of communism's ideological masquerade.

As an inverted and parodic *Bildungsroman*, *Velvet Tache* offers its readers the means to cope with Romania's nightmare of dictatorial ideology both through Tache's exploits and his engaging solidarity with his close friends, the trickster figures of Boyar Lăpai and especially the Dwarf. Even though their mischievous and sometimes magical exploits do not fully counter Mamona the Young and Vaucher's sadistic behavior and pathological egotism, such attempts legitimize the feelings of helplessness and confusion that many of Agopian's readers must have experienced on a daily basis, and make such feelings and disillusionment more bearable. It seems that Agopian's magic, which exaggerates the horrors of reality, serves that exact function. It helps his readers transcend reality and look at their lives from a different perspective, and then find something redeeming, and even hope, in even the worst situations.

While reconstructing historical events, Tache's extraordinary narrative bridges the two worlds – one of Mălura and the other of communist Romania – that are transparently analogous in terms of their respective referencing of reality. As an historical memoir reflecting a harsh time that reminds the readers, through Tache's otherworldly perspective, that no social order is infallible, Velvet Tache also provides its readers with a way to engage in a communal self-reflection when faced with the burden of unbearable situations, allows them to redefine themselves spiritually and intellectually as they escape into a different, fictional realm, and inspires them to negotiate some sort of protection from a magical world in the face of current adversity.

Ileana Alexandra Orlich

NOTES: INTRODUCTION

[1]Tzara's name was Samuel Rosenstock, but his pen name ("tzara," which means *motherland* in Romanian, and "Tristan," which means *sad*) was meant to connect him to a defining identity.

[2]Stoppard's play, which features James Joyce, Vladimir Ilych Lenin, and Tristan Tzara as quintessential figures of the twentieth century, uses humorous allusions and adapted quotes from Tzara's "Lampisteries précedée des sept manifestes dada" (Paris: 1963) and from Tzara's collected observations, suggestively titled "*Le pouvoir des images*."

[3]Eugen Lovinescu, Istoria *literaturii române contemporane* 6 vols. (Bucureşti: Anchora, 1926), 29. *Istoria literaturii române contemporane*, 1900-1937 (Bucureşti: Socec, 1937).

[4]George Călinescu, Istoria *literaturii române de la origini până in present*, (Bucureşti: Fundaţia Regală pentru Literatură, şi Artă, 1941).

[5]Gellu Naum's poetry was published in the volumes *The Firing Traveler* (1936); *The Freedom to Sleep on a Forehead* (1937); *Vasco de Gama* (1940); *The Corridor of Sleep* (1944); *Medium* (1945); *The Terrible Forbidden* (1945); *The Blind Man's Castle* (1946). Of these, the 1936 and 1937 volumes were illustrated by Brauner.

[6]*The Irigaray Reader*, ed. Margaret Whitford, (Oxford: Blackwell, 1991), 144.

[7]According to Peggy Guggenheim, there was a row at a Surrealist party that ended with Brauner losing his eye, even though the painter had been an innocent onlooker. Dominguez, a surrealist painter, seized a bottle and hurled it at someone else, and it ended up shattering in Brauner's eye. After being taken to a hospital by his friends, surgery was performed to remove the pieces of glass and replace the eye. A glass eye was bought and Brauner began to paint again, and very well, once he healed completely, maintaining the prophetic quality that had inspired him to paint himself as missing one eye even before the accident. The eye is a recurring image in Brauner's work.

[8]The trilogy's novels in my translation are available as follows: *The Disheveled Maidens*, (Bucharest: The Romanian Cultural Institute Publishing House, 2004); *A Concert of Music by Bach*, (Craiova: Scrisul românesc, Fundaţia Editura, 2005); *The Hidden Way*, (Craiova, Scrisul românesc, Fundaţia Editura, 2007).

[9]Co-founded by Cezar Petrescu, Gib Mihăescu and Adrian Maniu, *Gândirea*, especially after 1926 when Nechifor Crainic became its sole director-editor, rejected "westernization" in favor of "autochthonism" and rural culture that promoted ethnocentric models of culture.

[10]Quoted in Dumitru Micu, Istoria *literaturii române: De la creaţia populară la post modernism* (*History of Romanian Literature: From Folk Creations to Post-Modernism*), Bucureşti: Saeculum I. O, 2000).

[11]Translations of Sadoveanu's novels are available as follows: *Tales from Ancuţa's Inns*, trans. Ileana Orlich, (Bucharest: The Romanian Cultural Institute Publishing House, 2004); *The Hatchet*, trans. Eugenia Farca, *Classics of Romanian Literature*, Volume III (New York: East European Monographs, 1991).

[12]Nicolae Manolescu, *Istoria critică a literaturii române* (Bucureşti: Minerva, 1990).

[13]David Bordwell, *Narration in the Fiction Film*, (Madison: University of Wisconsin Press, 1985).

[14]Ştefan Agopian, *Velvet Tache*, (Bucureşti: Paideia, 2008).

[15]Nicolae Bălescu, *Cuvânt preliminariu despre izvoarele istotiei românilor* (*Preliminary Word on the Sources of Romanian History*) (Bucureşti: Colegiul Naţional, 1845).

NOTES: CHAPTER 1

[1]Among notable views are Vasile Spiridon, "Despre 'poheticitatae' romanului"; Simona Popescu, "Salvarea specie. Despre suprarealism şi Gellu Naum" (Bucureşti: Editura Fundaţiei Culturale, 2000); Ovid S. Crohmălniceanu, *Plural: Culture and Civilization* Bucureşti:Institutul Cultural Român, 3 (19) 2003, 195-8. Of particular significance in this context is Monica Lovinescu's persuasive essay "*Est-etice/Unde scurte IV*," in which she argues against Marian Papahagi's view that Naum writes in the manner of Mircea Eliade's fantastic. Lovinescu's point is that Naum's surrealism is different from Eliade's fantastic, which attributes mythical approaches to daily occurrences.

[2]Interview with Simona Popescu, "*Suprarealism pe cont propriu*," Bucureşti: Editura Fundaţiei Culturale, 2000. (My translation)

[3]Iam borrowing this term from Ion Pop's chapter, "Prozopoeme," in his book, *Gellu Naum – poezia contra literaturii* (Casa Cărţii de Ştiinţă, Cluj, 2001). According to the Romanian critic, "Discursul său [al lui Naum] de narrator se desfăşoară de la început în vecinătatea poemelor, putând fi situate, ca la toţi avangardiştii, în zona de interferenţă dintre peomul în proză organizat pe o solidă armatură programatică de manifest" "Naum's narrative discourse takes place from the start on the margins of poetry, and thus can be located, as in the case of all avant-garde writers, on the border between prose and poetry built on a firm, manifesto-like foundation." 149 (My translation)

[4]Michel Beajour, "*Qu'est-ce que Nadja*?" *French Studies*, XX (1966), 366-387. In support of this view also see Vasile Spiridon's "Despre poheticitatea romanului."

[5]Carlos Lynes, "Surrealism and the Novel," *French Studies*, XX (1966), 366.

[6]I. A. Richards, "Critiques," *A Collection of Critical Essays on "The Waste Land,"* ed. Jay Martin, (Englewood Cliffs: Prentice Hall, 1968), 44.

[7]Jacob Korg, "Modern Art Techniques," *A Collection of Critical Essays on "The Waste Land,"* ed. Jay Martin, (Englewood Cliffs: Prentice Hall, 1968), 87.

[8]While the English novel frequently exploited the urban atmosphere (the examples of Gissing, Arthur Morrison, and Leonard Merrick,

to mention only a few of the urban novelists towards the end of the nineteenth century), English poets generally showed little awareness of urban life as poetic manner. Eliot, the poet of London, had to look for inspiration across the Channel where the French poets often testified to the hold which Paris exercised on them. Tèophile Gautier described the urban scene in "Paris" as "*...la ville.../Où de brouillards noyés les jours semblent des nuits,/Où parmis les toits bleus s'enchevêtre et se cogne/Un soleil terne et mort comme l'oeil d'un ivrogne*" and in the same poem, in verses anticipating Eliot's many years later in *The Waste Land*, "*Incroyable chaos,/Babel des nations.../Chaudière des damnés, cuve immense.../Perpétuel contraste, éternelle antithèse,/Paris, la bonne ville, ou plutôt la mauvaise...* ." *Poésies complètes*, I, Paris 1905, 110.

[9]As Robert Young and Keith Hollaman describe, the "irreducible" element or event is something that cannot be explained according to the laws of the universe as they have been formulated empirically in Western discourse, that is, according to "logic, familiar knowledge, or received belief," *Magical Realist Fiction: An Anthology*, (New York: Longman, 1984).

[10]Tristan Tzara, *Lampisteries precédées des sept manifestes dada*, (Paris, 1963), 27.

[11]Tzara's name change (Tzara means "motherland" in Romanian) was meant to connect him to the idea of a defining identity. The adoption of a pseudonym has to be taken seriously in the case of the poet who confesses in "Approximate Man:" "On all the curves of the earth I've skated elegantly free/pressing to my bosom my destiny in monogram." Even after 1920, when he settled in Paris and was already famous, Tzara continued to write in Romanian and to send poems to be published in the "motherland."

[12]An interesting view of Tzara's radical ideas appears in Tom Stoppard's *Travesties*. In the play, Stoppard humorously sums up Tzara's exalted speeches that, in the spirit of the Dadaists, turn the artist into a militant revolutionary figure: "Now we need vandals and desecrators, simple-minded demolition men to smash centuries of baroque subtleties, to bring down the temple and thus finally to reconcile the shame and the necessity of being an artist! Dada! Dada!" (62).

[13]Robert Motherwell, *The Dada Painters and Poets: An Anthology* (New York: New York: Wittenborn, Schultz, 1951). 53-54.

[14]Alongside the "Dada is always wrong," consider, for instance, Tzara's proclamation: "Dada remains in the European frame of weakness, all of it shitty, but we want henceforth to shit in various colors in order to decorate the zoo of art with the flag of all embassies." *Lampisteries precédées des sept manifestes dada* (Paris, 1963), 15.

[15]Eliot, "Four Elizabethan Dramatists," *Selected Essays of T. S. Eliot*, (New York: Harcourt Brace & World, 1964), 93.

[16]For more information on these journals see the Introduction.

[17]Andre Breton, "Second Manifesto of Surrealism," in *Manifestoes of Surrealism*, trans. Richard Seaver and Helen R. Lane, (Ann Arbor: University of Michigan Press, 1969), 123-24.

[18]James Brook and Sasha Vlad, translators (Evanston: Northwestern University Press, 1995). All quotes are from this edition of *Zenobia.*

[19]See Benjamin (Fundoianu) Fondane's "Prefaţa" (Preface) to his volume *Privelişti*, which includes poems written between 1917 and 1923 that made a great impact on the newer generation of Romanian surrealist. Titled *Câteva cuvinte pădurete*, which loosely translated means "words as tart as green apples." The "Prefaţa" advises young poets that artistic creation must not be mawkish and follow convention, but instead should use words that sting the taste buds, like the tart green apples, suggested in the Preface title.

[20]In this issue, see Breton's "Les Vases communicants" (1932), in which he reiterates that the aim of Surrealism was "to throw a *conducting wire* between the too much dissociated worlds of waking and sleep, of exterior and interior reality, of reason and madness, of the calm of knowledge and of love." It is from the bringing together of such states that special images form to reveal a contrast between the everyday world and the world of dream or madness, a moment of interchange between the conscious and subconscious mind. Similar views are forwarded in other writings, such as "What is Surrealism" (1934), in which Breton addresses various definitions of the movement at a time when the surrealist movement was widely embraced in the artistic circles.

[21]Ovid S. Crohmălniceanu, "Gellu Naum 1915-2001," in *Plural: Hot Black Ink: Modernist Idiosyncracies: Urmuz, Mateiu, Blechner, Fondane, Naum*, (Bucharest: The Romanian Cultural Institute, 3 (19) 2003), 197.

[22]Germán List Arzubide, *El movimiento estridentista* (Jalalpa: Horizonte, 1927), 40-41.

[23]André Breton,*Nadja*, trans. Richard Howard. (New York: Grove Press, 1960). All quotations are from this edition.

[24]See James' letter to Mrs. Humphrey Ward (July 26, 1899), *Letters*, Vol. 4, 111.

[25]Ralph Waldo Emerson, "Uses of Great Men" and "Nominalist and Realist," respectively.

[26]James Brook, "*Contestarea poetică. Interviu cu Gellu Naum*," *Observatorul Cultural* Nr. 1, 2000.

[27]Xavière Gauthier, *Surréalisme et sexualité*.

[28]*French Studies*, XX (1966), 366-387.

[29]Bethany Ladimer, "Madness and the Irrational in the Works of André Breton: A Feminist Perspective," in *Feminist Studies*, Vol. 6, No. 1, Spring 1980, 175-95.

[30]See "Women and Madness: The Critical Phallacy," in which Felman offers a lucid discussion of the implications of this basic Western philosophical principle of woman's otherness/femininity mirroring the masculine side/masculinity. In contemporary French critical terminology, this reassuring definition of femininity as a constant reminder of masculinity is often named "the Other(ness)" of woman because it functions as a sort of mirror or reflector (of masculinity).

[31]Ion Pop, *Gellu Naum – poezia contra literaturii*, (Cluj: Casa Cartii de Stiinta, 2001), 163.

[32]Here, I am using F. H. Bradley's concept of the Absolute as the sum total of all experiences, which Eliot appropriated as the underlining view of *The Waste Land*. For a more detailed discussion of this plot, see Jewel Spears Brooker and Joseph Bentley, "Unifying Incompatible Worlds: The Sybil of Cumae and Tiresias" in *Reading The Waste Land: Modernism and the Limits of Interpretation* (Amherst: University of Massachusetts Press, 1990), 14-34.

[33]The first translation of T. S. Eliot's poems into Romanian was T. S. Eliot, *Poezii*, (Bucureşti: Editura pentru literatură, 1965), trans. Ion Pillat. Another translation of Eliot's poems by Aurel Covaci appeared in 1970 (Bucureşti: Editura Albatros).

[34]This point, which is also made in John Xiros Cooper's *T. S. Eliot and The Politics of Voice* (Ann Arbor: UMI Research Press, 1987) 58, of the deeper level of coherence and intelligibility, where fragmented and alienated consciousness coalesces into "natural" unities, Eliot himself describes in "*The Use of Poetry and the Use of Criticism* (1933), as a level where the speaking voice enacts the deepest feeling for syllable and rhythm, penetrating far below the conscious levels of thought and feeling, invigorating every word; sinking into to the most primitive and forgotten, returning to the origins and bringing something back, seeking the beginning and the end. It works through meanings, certainly, or not without meanings in the ordinary sense, and fuses the old and obliterated into the trite, the current, and the new and surprising, the most ancient and the most civilized mentality. What Eliot argues here, that the penetrative processes described are neither unconscious nor blind, but highly conscious, motivated and meant to violently contest an affective terrain dominated by romantic forms of inwardness, is also Naum's (and the Surrealists') point and protests in *Zenobia.*

[35]Convincingly, Tate argues that "there is no despair in the scene itself" and that the critics who "are necessarily blind to an effect of irony, have mistaken the symbols of an ironic contrast for the terms of philosophic dilemma...The clerk stands for the secularization of the religious and quantitative values in the modern world...The meaning of the contrast between the clerk and Tiresias is not disillusion, but irony. The scene is a masterpiece, perhaps the most profound vision we have of modern man." "The Fire Sermon," in *A Collection of Critical Essays on "The Waste Land,"* ed. Jay Martin (Englewood Cliffs: Prentice Hall, 1968), 32-3.

[36]I am thinking of Woolf's well-known description of the young woman and young man coming from opposite sides of the street to enter a London taxi, which thereby symbolically becomes the space of the androgynous mind, composed of both female and male personae.

[37]See Marian Papahagi, "*In căutarea sensului ascuns*," in *Cumpănă şi semn* (Bucureşti: Cartea românească, 1990), 36-42.

[38]Julia Kristeva, *Revolution in Poetic Language*, trans. Margaret Waller (New York: Columbia University Press, 1984), esp. 21-30.

[39]For a detailed analysis of Eliot's cubistic portraits of women in *The Waste Land*, see Jewel Spears Brooker Reading *The Waste Land: Modernism and the Limits of Interpretation* (Amherst: The University of Massachusetts, 1990), 95.

[40]Ion Pop, *Gellu Naum – poezia contra literaturii*, (Cluj: Casa Cărţii de Ştiinţă, 2001), 165.

[41]Marian Papahagi, "*In căutarea sensului ascuns*," in *Cumpănă şi semn* (Bucureşti: Cartea românească, 1990), 36-42.

[42]Christine Buci-Glucksmann, *Baroque Reason: The Aesthetics of Modernity*, trans. Patrick Camiller (London: Sage, 1994), 49.

[43]Breton, "A Letter to Seers," in *Manifestoes of Surrealism*, trans. Richard Seaver and Helen R. Lane (Ann Arbor: University of Michigan Press, 1969), 197.

[44]Luce Irigaray, *The Irigaray Reader*, ed. Margaret Whitford (Oxford: Blackwell, 1991), 144.

[45]Luce Irigaray, "La Mystérique," in *Speculum of Another Woman*, trans. Gillian C. Gill (Ithaca: Cornell University Press, 1984), 191-202.

NOTES: CHAPTER 2

[1]Space will not allow me to enumerate the great number of short, disparate articles from literary journals and newspapers that mention Camil Petrescu's indebtedness to Proust. As a synthesis of such views, mention needs to be made however of the respected critic Paul Georgescu's lengthy analysis in two essays, "Frumusețea adevărului" (The Beauty of Truth) and "Clasicismul creator" (Creative Classicism), both included in his critical volume *Printre cărți* (Among books). (București: Editura Eminescu, 1973), 86-92, 93-99. After discussing the numerous similarities between the two novelists, Georgescu's commentary emphasizes the different scope of Petrescu's novel, which, unlike the Proustian narratives, dramatizes first and foremost a panoramic view of the Romanian society between the two wars.

[2]*Between Men: English Literature and Male Homosocial Desire*, (New York: Columbia University Press, 1985,)1.

[3]All citations are from *The Bed of Procrustes*, trans. Ileana Alexandra Orlich, (Bucharest: Editura Fundația Camil Petrescu, 2008). [Since the Romanian version of "Procrustes" is "*Procust*" I decided to leave the form Procustes in my translation.]

[4]George Călinescu, *Istoria Literaturii române* (History of Romanian Literature), trans. Leon Levițchi, (Milan: UNESCO NAGARD Publishers, 1988), 627.

[5]Remy de Gourmont, *Natural Philosophy of Love*, trans. With a postscript by Ezra Pound. (New York: privately printed for Rarity Press, 1931), 169.

[6]T. S. Eliot, "Hamlet and His Problems," in *The Sacred Wood and Major Early Essays*, (New York: Dover Publications, Inc., 1998), 58.

[7]As Director of the National Theatre in Bucharest, Camil Petrescu was very engaged in the cultural scene, which was heavily influenced by Western art and literature. In 1947, he became a member of the Romanian Academy, a status that acknowledged at the highest level his involvement in Romania's cultural dialogue with the West.

[8]Eliot's portraits of women, which suffered great changes after Ezra Pound's cuts in Eliot's manuscripts, include such "types" as the "plain simple bitch" and the "strolling slattern in a tawdry gown." For a detailed list, see T. S. Eliot, *The Waste Land: A Facsimile and Transcript of the Original Drafts, ed. Valerie Eliot*, (London: Fa-

ber and Faber, 1971), 27.

[9]Sandra M. Gilbert and Susan Gubar, *No Man's Land: The Place of the Woman Writer in the Twentieth Century* vol. 2. (New Haven: Yale University Press, 1989), 260.

[10]Once again, space will not allow me to mention the numerous names of critics who regarded Ladima as a victim of capitalism, a latter-day Bartleby of the journalistic world. Chief among such views is Sorin Arghir's commentary in his "Preface" to the Year Edition of *Patul lui Procust*, (Bucureşti: Editura de Stat pentru Literatură şi Artă, 1957). Arghir writes: "Prin Ladima, Camil Petrescu infăţişează, de fapt, tipul proletarului intellectual, prezintă condiţia de viaţă a acestuia în societatea burgheză." (Through Ladima's character, Camil Petrescu portrays, in fact, the intellectual, proletarian type, presents his [the intellectual's] living conditions in a bourgeois society.) (my translation)

[11]Huge snakes devoured by bed bugs.

[12]T. S. Eliot, "Lecture I: Toward a Definition of a Metaphysical Poetry," The *Varieties of Metaphysical Poetry*, ed. Ronald Schuchard, (New York: Harcourt Brace and Company, 1993), 227.

[13]Eliot, "Milton II." Selected *Prose of T. S. Eliot*, ed. Frank Kermode, (New York: Harcourt Trade, 1975) 266.

[14]Eliot, "Tradition and Individual Talent," *The Sacred Wood*, 31.

[15]Quoted in Havelock Ellis, *Studies in the Psychology of Sex*. Vol. I (Philadelphia: F. A. Davis Company, Publishers, 1913), 219.

[16]Ibid.

[17]Charles Baudelaire, "The Painter of Modern Life," *Les Fleurs du Mal*, trans. C. F. MacIntyre, (Brekeley: University of California Press, 1947), 105.

[18]Fundamental to Pound's prototypic Imagist poem "In a Station of the Metro," the compressed images result from the copulation of two depictable images in a visual metamorphosis that gives birth to a disembodied observer.

[19]I am borrowing the term from Peter Nicholls, *Modernism: A Literary Guide*, (Berkeley: University of California Press, 1995), 3.

[20]Sigmund Freud, "The Interpretation of Dreams," (1900), in *The Standard Edition of the Complete Psychological Works* 4, 149.

[21]Lotte H. Eisner, *The Haunted Screen: Expressionism in the German Cinema and the Influence of Max Reinhardt*, trans. Roger Greaves, (London: Thames and Hudson, 1969), 15.

[22]T. S. Eliot, The *Complete Poems and Plays* 1909-1950, (New York: Harcourt, Brace and Company, 1958), 19. (Hereafter cited as CPP)

NOTES: CHAPTER 3

[1]All three novels were read in installments, while being written, during the literary soirées of the literary cénacle Sburătorul.

[2]T. S. Eliot, "The Metaphysical Poets" (1921), *Selected Prose of T. S. Eliot*, ed. Frank Kermode, (New York: Harcourt Trade, 1975), 66.

[3]Mini's passing in review of Bucharest's well-known landmarks is not unlike the lengthy city descriptions in Theodore Dreiser's *Sister Carrie* (1900), another novel which details the location and nature of Chicago and New York theatres, restaurants, hotels, and major streets and to which *The Disheveled Maidens* bears more than a casual resemblance. Apart from more tangible similarities, the two novels that were written only two decades apart also share two strikingly evident paradoxes: (1) a solid, self-conscious attempt to anchor their narrative in early-twentieth-century Romanian and American life, which ultimately succeeds in foregrounding their modernity; and (2) the power and endurance of both novels, in spite of what critics at large have often considered to be an awkward and inept prose style.

[4]My translation of the title in English, *The Disheveled Maidens*, takes into account the Middle English disheveled, from Old French *deschevele*, past principle of *descheveler*, to disarrange the hair: *des* – apart; *dis + chevel* (hair, from Latin *capillus*). Disheveled, according to Webster's *Unabridged Dictionary* (1996) is 1. Having in loose disorder; disarranged; as disheveled hair. 2. Having the hair in loose disorder as in "The dancing maidens are disheveled Maenads." – J. A. Symonds.

[5]This view is generally embraced by most Romanian critics who follow the respected George Călinescu's view that Papadat-Bengescu's writings are "an essentially feminine literature, with no exit from the close circuit of the sexual condition … The life of the senses … with implicit confidence in these values, are the only aspects with which she deals extensively. What a woman feels physically when she is in good health or taken ill, how she wants or repudiates a man … these are the writer's themes." *History of Romanian Literature*, trans. Leon Levițchi (Milan: UNESCO NAGARD Publishers, 1988) 627.

[6]I am using here Gert Buelens definition in "Henry James's Oblique Possession: Plottings of Desire and Mastery in *The American Scene*," *PMLA* 116 2 (March 2001): 300-13.

[7]For a detailed discussion of this view, see Aaron Betsky, *Build-*

ing Sex: Men, Women, Architecture, and the Construction of Sexuality (New York: William Morrow and Company, Inc., 1995). Betsky's point is certainly echoed in *Sister Carrie*, where the heroine manages to create a powerful space for herself as another person who is the very embodiment of the city. Her ability to buy into and re-create the realm to which women are assigned and through which they define themselves enables her to make her way in the city, first Chicago and then New York. By the end of the book she has become an actress, in complete control of her destiny in and through the city that is her stage.

[8]Reed, who made Bucharest his headquarters for ventures into the WWI zones in neighboring Serbia, Russia, Bulgaria and Turkey, made the infamous comment in a letter sent to his friend and former professor Charles Copeland.

[9]Rosa Goldsmith, a.k.a. Countess Waldeck, first published *Athéné Palace* in 1942 (New York: Robert M. McBride & Co). The book received excellent critical attention. *The Christian Science Monitor* called it "a spicy record of observations made in one of the world's most volatile of social and diplomatic populations." (May 29, 1942): 12. Recently, *Athéné Palace*, (Iaşi: The Center for Romanian Studies, 1998), was published in Romania, with excellent notes, comments and introduction by Ernest H. Latham.

[10]For a detailed discussion of these issues see K. Peiss, "Making Up and Making Over: Cosmetics, Consumer Culture, and Women's Identity," in *The Sex of Things: Gender and Consumption in Historical Perspective*, ed. V. de Grazia. (Berkeley, CA: University of California Press), 311-36.

[11]Although I am borrowing the term (see Karen Halttuten, *Confidence Men and Painted Women: A Study of Middle-Class Culture in America*, 1830-1870 ([New Haven: Yale UP, 1982]), I would like to emphasize that in the Romanian language this is precisely the word used to designate women wearing excessive make up, "*femei pictate*."

[12]The legend says that Bucharest was founded by a shepherd named Bucur; another variant, more likely, is that it was established by Mircea cel Bătrân in the fourteenth century after a victory over the Turks (*bucurie* means joy in Romanian, which is why Bucharest is often called "The City of Joy"). Bucharest is first mentioned under its current name as a residence during the reign of Vlad Ţepes (Vlad the Impaler) in a 1459 court document. It soon became the summer residence of the court. In 1595 it was burned by the Turks; but, after

its restoration, it continued to grow in size and prosperity. In 1698 Prince Constantin Brâncoveanu chose it for his capital. After the unification of the Romanian provinces Walachia and Moldavia in 1859, Bucharest became the capital of the Romanian state declared in 1861. In the second half of the nineteenth century, the population of the city increased dramatically. The extravagant architecture and cosmopolitan high culture of this period won Bucharest the nickname of Paris of the East (or little Paris), with Calea Victoriei as its Champs Elysée.

[13]The folk ballad *Master Builder Manole* has traditionally been interpreted as "a portrait of the artist forced to sacrifice the woman he loves for the sake of his art." For a different point of view in the interpretation of this enduring literary masterpiece of Romanian folk tradition, see the chapter "Master Builder Manole" in my book *Silent Bodies: (Re)Discovering the Women of Romanian Short Fiction*, (New York: Columbia University Press, 2002).

[14]I am indebted to Richard Poirier, who uses this formulation in "Panoramic Environment and the Anonymity of the Self," Theodore Dreiser, *Sister Carrie*, ed. Donald Pizer, Norton Critical Edition. (New York: Norton, 1970), 583.

[15]I quote from Hebbel's preface to *Maria Magdalena*. References to Hebbel's works, translated by Carl Richard Mueller, are to *Masterpieces of the Modern German Theatre*, ed. Robert W. Corrigan, (New York: Collier, 1967).

[16]For an interesting discussion on Hebbel's influence of Ibsen, see Joan Templeton, "Fallen Women and Upright Wives: "Women's Place in Early Modern Tragedy," *Reconfigured Spheres: Feminist Explorations of Literary Spaces*, eds. Margaret R. Higonnet and Joan Templeton, (Amherst: University of Massachussetts Press, 1994), 60-71.

[17]I am using Elaine Showalter's formulation defined in *Sexual Anarchy, Gender and Culture at the Fin de Siécle*. (London, 1995).

[18]This view is not embraced by most Romanian critics who generally follow the respected view of George Călinescu that Papadat-Bengescu's writings are "an essentially feminine literature, with no exit from the close circuit of the sexual condition ... The life of the senses ... with implicit confidence in these values, are the only aspects with which she deals extensively. What a woman feels physically when she is in good health or taken ill, how she wants or repudiates a man ... these are the writer's themes." *History of Romanian Litera-*

ture, trans. Leon Leviţchi, (Milan, UNESCO NAGARD Publishers, 1988), 627.

[19]Adrienne Rich, "Notes toward a Politics of Location," *Blood, Bread and Poetry: Selected Prose* 1979-1985, (New York: W. W. Norton & Company, 1986).

[20]Although my use here of the term subaltern should be taken in its general sense of subordinate, it owes much to Gayatri Chakravorty Spivak's notion of subaltern as "excluded" and "not legitimized" in "Can the Subaltern Speak?" *Marxism and the Interpretation of Culture*, eds. Cary Nelson and Lawrence Grossberg, (Urbana, IL: University of Illinois Press, 1988).

[21]Martin Lamm, *Modern Drama*, trans. Karen Elliott, (New York: Philosophical Library, 1953), 14.

[22]Robert Gaines, *Evening in the Palace of Reason*, (New York: Harper Collins Publishers, 2005), 115.

[23]Ibid, 304.

[24]For an elaborate discussion of this point, see Joan Wallach Scott, "Gender: A Useful Category of Historical Analysis" in *Gender and Politics of History*, (New York: Columbia University Press, 1988), 28-50.

[25]Judith P. Butler, *Gender Trouble: Feminism and the Subversion of Identity*, (New York, Routledge, 1990). See also her essay "Imitation and Gender Insubordination," in *Inside/Out: Lesbian Theories, Gay Theories*, ed. Diana Fuss, (New York: Routledge, 1991), 13-31.

[26]Betty Fridan, *The Feminine Mystique*, (New York: Dell Books, 1963).

[27]For an interesting view of feminine/masculine opposition in music see Suzanne Cusick, "Feminist Theory, Music Theory, and the Mind/Body Problem" in *Perspectives of New Music*, Vol. 32, No. 1 (Winter, 1994), 8-27.

[28]In an interview published in *Lumea românească* (October 12, 1928), Papadat-Bengescu discusses the difficulty of finding a suitable title. She also remarks that, although the title of the first novel, *The Disheveled Maidens* (Fecioarele despletite), was somewhat vague and the title of the second, *A Concert of Music by Bach* (Concert din

Muzică de Bach), was a very solid one, the third novel's title emerged after many indecisions and endless deliberations.

[29]In another interview with I. Valerian immediately after the publication of *A Concert of Music by Bach*, Papadat-Bengescu mentions that she is working on two other novels, one of which is clearly *The Hidden Way.* An entire chapter titled "Doctor Walter" was published as early as December 1926 in the pages of *Sburătorul* (an IV), and then another long chapter titled "Coca-Aimée" was published in the same journal a year later, in 1927. Another friend of Papadat-Bengescu, the writer and critic Camil Baltazar, also published a chapter of the third novel of the trilogy in 1927 in his own journal, *Tiparnița literară*, under the title *Drumuri care nu se văd* (Roads that cannot be seen), the same tentative title the writer had in mind before deciding on The Hidden Way. Although the novel was completed in 1929, it was not published until 1932. The delay resulted from the bankruptcy of the writer's good friend S. Benvenisti, who had published for many years the works of the members of *Sburătorul*, and with Papadat-Bengescu's own lack of connections with the publishers of the day. Finally, Camil Baltazar directed hr toward S. Ciornei, who published *The Hidden Way* at his own press, *Editura Națională*.

[30]*The Hidden Way* intrigued and disappointed some of the critics who had previously praised Papadat-Bengescu's works, especially the first two novels of the trilogy. Among her notable critics are Mihail Sebastian, who writes that the novel is "an abstract perfection," but that precisely for this reason it lacks the warmth necessary to great artistic creation; George Călinescu, who also comments on the cold quality of the narrative and states that the world of *The Hidden Way* is "hideous." (*Adevărul literar și artistic*. Seria II, an X, 22, May 1932, 7); and Eugen Ionesco, who declared that in *No* that *The Hidden Way* does not belong to Papadat-Bengescu, that she simply borrowed it from French literature and added "some worn-out and patched up French masks to the faces of Romanian fictional characters." An exception to these negative views was Anton Holban, who praises the novel as the best of the entire trilogy (*Azi*, an I, no. 3-4, 1932). He also ranks *The Hidden Way* with Thomas Mann's *The Magic Mountain*, another work that uses as locale a sanatorium and focuses primarily on the topics of life and death, and declares it a greater work than that of André Gide, whose portrayal of perverse adolescents pales by comparison with Papadat-Bengescu's Coca-Aimée.

[31]In addressing the relation of embodiment to representation, it is important to keep in mind Montaigne's position, which Papadat-Bengescu seems to have appropriated. In Montaigne's *Essays*, knowledge is embodied, not only because it takes as its horizon the

live, experiential body, but also because of its terminology and meaning are situated within representation. The body is not independent of the ways of knowing but attains embodiment through them. Its materiality is not a given, since it is constituted provisionally through representations, understood as a material signifying process.

[32]Derived from Latin, the Romanian word *cultura* also means agricultural cultivation. Given Papadat-Bengescu's fictional use of the body, her claims for the cultivation of the body, which include and imply the cultivation of the body in the physical and moral sense, would also entail her emphasis on the formative character of cultural determinations.

[33]Merleau-Ponty, *The Phenomenology of Perception*, trans. Colin Smith, (London: Routledge and Kegan Paul, 1995), 408.

[34]In his note "Flesh of the World – Flesch of the Body – Being" (May 1960), Merleau-Ponty explains that while the flesh of the body is self-sensing, the flesh of the world is "sensible and not sentient." He emphasizes that it is by the flesh of the world that one can understand the living body. *The Visible and the Invisible*, trans. Alphonso Lingis, (Evanston: Northwest University Press, 1968), 248-50.

[35]For further theorizing of this point, see Kristeva's Powers *of Horror: An Essay in Abjection*, trans. Leon S. Roudiez, (New York: Columbia University Press, 1983), 18, 20. Destroying the Law of the Father in order to release anarchic, liberating *jouissance* has long been theorized positively, as by Marcuse in *Eros and Civilization* in "The Father's 'No'" and "Revolutionary Action: 'Until Now'" (218-33).

[36]Papadat-Bengescu's emphasis on the role of art as a redemptive force is certainly in line with the views of her contemporaries. It has been recently argued that, by the turn of the century, aesthetic appreciation and strong new market for antiques, be they the antiquities of Greece and Rome sought by collectors or just the old household items perceived as better, were enhanced by claims that such *objects d'art* could serve as a haven for city inhabitants like the inhabitants of Bucharest, that they provided the ultimate safety zone where urban filth could be kept at bay.

[37]Judith Butler, Gender *Trouble: Feminism and the Subversion of Identity*, (New York: Routledge, 1999).

[38]George Bernard Shaw, *Heartbreak House* (Harmondsworth: Penguin, 1964), 127.

[39]I am indebted for this formulation to Dalia Judovitz's discussion of similar issues in *The Culture of the Body: Genealogies of Modernity*, (Ann Arbor: The University of Michigan Press, 2004).

[40]Quoted in Susan Sontag's *Illness as Metaphor*, (New York: Farrar, Straus and Giroux, 1978), 43.

[41]Luce Irigaray, *Ce sexe qui n'en est pas un*, (Paris: Minuit, 1977), 134.

[42]Toril Moi, *Sexual Textual Politics*, (London: Routledge, 1985), 140.

[43]*Ce sexe qui n'en est pas un*, 134.

[44]The urgent new agenda in the representation of the body occurring immediately after or around the First World War finds a resonant echo in Virginia Woolf's 1926 essay "On Being Ill." Her observation on how "All day all night the body intervenes," ... though "of all this daily drama of the body there is no record". *The Essays of Virginia Woolf, Volume IV* (1925-1928), (London: Hogarth Press, 1986), 317-8, may well be the outcome of the WWI itself, with its dehumanized and industrial technologies of trench, tanks and war planes symbolically smashing bodies like that of D. H. Lawrence's Clifford Chatterly. In the same train of thought, one can also print to J. D.'s 1919 essay "Notes on Thought and Vision" that uses the body as center of consciousness when she says "Our concern is with the body." *The Gender of Modernism*, ed. Bonnie Kime Scott, (Bloomington: Indiana University Press, 1990), 108.

[45]Hilda's German roots do seem to be an accidental fiction. In her essay "Silenced Women in the Grimm Tales: The 'Fit' between Fairy Tales and Society in Their Historical Context," Ruth B. Bottigheimer notes the significance of female submission in disparate areas of German life. She attributes submission to the Grimm Brothers stories (very popular in Romania and certainly familiar to Papadat-Bengescu as a woman and mother who brought up five children), that she finds responsible for propagating among the young readers obedient types of women as model heroines. *Fairy Tales and Society: Illusion, Allusion, and Paradigm*. Ed. Ruth B. Bottigheimer. (Philadelphia: University of Pennsylvania Press, 1986), 115-131.

[46]See especially Eugenia Tudor Anton's discussion of *The Hidden Way in Drumul ascuns*, "Postfaţa," (Bucureşti: Minerva, 1985).

[47]In his study of *Drumul ascuns* (The Hidden Way), "Armonii statice şi necesare," Valeriu Râpeanu praises Elena and all the femine

characters in the novel. He also asserts that all the male characters are weak and simply puppets in the hands of the powerful women in the novel. *Drumul ascuns: Prefaţă, Curriculum vitae şi Bibliografie*, (Bucureşti: Editura 100+1 Gramar, 1990).

NOTES: CHAPTER 4

[1]Walter J. Ong, Orality *and Literacy: The Technologizing of the World.* (New York: Routledge, 1982).

[2]Brian V. Street, *Literacy in Theory and Practice*, (Cambridge: Cambridge UP, 1984), 110.

[3]Nicolae Iorga, *Istoria Literaturii in secolul al XVIII-lea*, 1901. 2 vol., (Bucharest: Minerva, 1901).

[4]Emil Cioran, *Breviaire de vaincus*, 1940-44, (Breviary of the Defeated), trans. Alain Paruit, Paris: Gallimard, 1993.

[5]Bălan, *Concise History of Romanian Literature*, trans. Andrei Bantaş, (Bucharest: Editura enciclopedică şi ştiinţifică, 1981).

[6]Constantin Ciopraga, *The Personality of Romanian Literature: A Synthesis*, trans. Ştefan Avădanei, (Iaşi: Junimea, 1991).

[7]Mircea Eliade, *The Fate of Romanian Culture*, trans. Bogdan Ştefănescu, (Bucureşti: Editura Athena, 1995).

[8]Ernest H. Latham, *Mioriţa: An Icon of Romanian Culture* (Iaşi: The Center for Romanian Studies, 1999). Quotations from the *Mioriţa* ballad are from this bilingual edition.

[9]Mihail Sadoveanu, *The Hatchet*, trans. Eugenia Farca, Classics *of Romanian Literature*, Volume III (New York: East European Monographs, 1991). All quotations are from this edition.

[10]Mircea Eliade, *Zamolxis, the Vanishing God*, trans. Willard Trask, (Chicago: University of Chicago Press, 1972).

[11]Lucian Blaga, *Spaţiul Mioritic Trilogia culturii*, (Bucureşti: Editura pentru Literatură Universală, 1969), 119-31.

[12]Vlad Georgescu, *The Romanians: A History*, ed. Matei Călinescu, trans. Alexandra Bley-Vroman, (Columbus: Ohio State Press, 1991), 205.

[13]Sadoveanu himself once described how he was inspired to write the story: while traveling around the country on a very hot day, he stopped at an inn to rest and to eat. At a nearby table he heard two policemen talking about a shepherd who had been killed and speculating as

to who the murderer might be. The incident, which made Sadoveanu recall the *Miorița* plot, cast a retrospective light on the old folk ballad, which found in *The Hatchet* its greatest literary expression.

[14]All quotations are from *Tales from Ancuța*'s Inn, trans. Ileana Alexandra Orlich, (Bucharest: Editura Institutului Cultural Roman, 2004). The *Tales* will be the shortened form of the novel's full title by which I will identify *Tales from Ancuța's Inn.*

[15]The unification of Wallachia (home province of the shepherd from Vrancea) and Moldovia in 1859 ended with national unification in 1918 when Transylvania (home to the Ungurean shepherd) was reunited with the other Romanian provinces in the aftermath of World War I.

[16]For an excellent critical commentary of the ballad, its history and cultural background, as well as an exquisite English translation complete with beautiful pictures illustrating the ballad's lines, see Ernest H. Latham, *Miorița: An Icon of Romanian Culture*, (Iași: The Center for Romanian Studies, 1999).

[17]Benedict Anderson, *Imagined Communities. Reflections on the Origins and Spread of Nationalism*, (London: Verso and New Left Books, 1983).

[18]This view is also expressed in George Călinescu's *Istoria literaturii române de la origini până in prezent* (București: Fundația Regală pentru Literatura și Artă, 1941).

[19]The word *Moș*, followed by a man's name, is a polite form of address in the rural areas of Romania, the equivalent of Old Man in English-speaking communities.

[20]My reference is to the trait of the grotesque which W. Kayser *in Das Grotesk in Malerei and Dichtung* identifies with its hostile and inhuman possibilities.

[21]Mircea Muthu, "'Haiducul' in literaturile sud-europene," (" The Haiduk in East-European Literature") *Revista de istorie și teorie literară* 32.3 (July-September, 1984), 68-73.

[22]A *Comis*, was a ranking official in Moldavia, similar to an equerry, whose position corresponded to that of a squire. Such a person was usually chosen from among the freemen, or free landholders, called *răzăși*.

[23]Roland Barthes, *The Pleasures of the Text*, (New York: Farrar, 1975).

NOTES: CHAPTER 5

[1] *Velvet Tache* (*Tache de catifea*) was published in Bucureşti, Romania by Editura Românească in 1981. Although the publication did not attract special attention, the respected critic Paul Georgescu praised the book. In the leading literary journal *Romania literară*, Georgescu called Agopian "an excellent story teller, with remarkable individual style, unmatched by any else's" and stated that *Velvet Tache* calls for the highest praise. The quotes used in this essay are from the English edition of *Velvet Tache*, trans. Ileana Alexandra Orlich, (Bucureşti: Paideia, 2008).

[2]Among the critics voicing such views are the respected Mircea Mihăieş, Dan C. Mihăilescu, and Eugen Negrici.

[3]The seminal works that began the process of defining magical realism, Franz Roh's "Magic Realism: Post Expressionists" and Alejo Carpentier's "On the Marvelous Real in America" and "The Baroque and the Marvelous Real," were followed by much scholarship that continued in developing the definition of the genre. Of these, mention needs to be made of Wendy Faris's essay, "Scheherazade's Children: Magical Realism and Postmodern Fiction," in her collection of essays of the same title, and of her more recent book, *Ordinary Enchantments: Magical Realism and the Remystification of Narrative*, in which Faris claims that magical realism is the most important contemporary trend in international fiction. Expressing the collective sentiment about the critical production of "magic realist" writing, Peter Hulme has succinctly described it as "a hyper reality of international proportions," "Introduction," *Discourse/Postcolonial Theory*, (Manchester: Manchester University Press, 1994), 14.

[4]Linda Kenyon, "A Conversation with Robert Kroetsch," *New Quarterly* 5, (Spring 1985): 15. See also Stanley McMullin, "'Adam's Mad in Eden': Magic Realism as Hinterland Experience" (in Hinchcliffe and Jewinski 13-22), who reads magic realism as implicitly "ex-centric."

[5]For this point , see Stephen Slemon's detailed argument that the marginal cultures' history of construction relies on the incorporation of literary texts of Western European provenance in the literary writings of marginal literatures, thus forcing the capacities of the major literary systems to come to terms with them. Stephen Slemon, "Magic Realism as Postcolonial Discourse," *Canadian Literature 116* (Spring, 1988): 9-24.

[6]My analysis follows closely Alfred J. Lopez's view that regards

the magic in magic realism as indigenous and established genres, like realism or romance, as Western. See Alfred J. Lopez, *Posts and Pasts: A Theory of Postcolonialism*, (Albany, SUNY Press, 2001).

[7]See Michel Valdez Moses, "Magic Realism at World's End," *Literary Imagination: The Review of the Association of Literary Scholars and Critics* 3 (2001(: 105-33.

[8]See José Monléon, *A Specter is Haunting Europe: A Sociohistorical Approach to the Fantastic*.

[9]Northrop Frye, *The Secular Scripture*, Cambridge, (Mass: Harvard University Press 1976).

[10]Eugen Negrici, "Prefaţa", to *Tache de catifea*, (Bucureşti: Polirom, 2004), 5-11.

[11]In his lecture of "Magical Realism in Spanish American Fiction," to the 1954 Congress of the Modern Languages Association in New York, subsequently published in *Hispania* 38, 2 (May 1955), Flores gave a definition of magical realism that departed from its original formulation. According to Flores, magical realism employs apparently reliable, realistic description of impossible or fantastic events and thus allows for the interchangeability of the terms magical realism *lo real maravilloso* and *el realismo maravilloso*. In 1967, attempting to return to the original formula of *el realismo maravilloso*, the Mexican critic Luis Real argues that the writer of magic realist texts uncovers the mystery hidden in ordinary objects and everyday reality.

[12]In this regard, Agopian follows the dictates of Romanian historians who traditionally valorize past and present from the perspective of a future that must preserve the past experiences and turn them to good and moral account. As Pavel Chihaia explains, this sort of "historicism" of the present for the future can be found in "the adaptation of the religious canonical themes found in the mural painting of Romanian churches to the social and political events of their time." *Arta medievală II. Invăţături şi mituri in Ţara Românească*, (Bucureşti: Albatros, 1998), 223.

[13]For a detailed exemplification of the term, see Laura Zăvăleanu's "A Descent into the Field of Histories: Between the Strictures of Science and the Generosity of Myth." *Transylvanian Review*, Vol. XV, No. 3, Fall 2006.

[14]This possibility gives further credence to Seymore Menton's assertion that the magical realism of the 1918-1981 period was both an expression, and, as I will show later, an alternative to existential anguish, for *Velvet Tache*'s author and for all those who lived in Ceausescu's Romania. See Seymor Menton's *Magic Realism Rediscovered: 1918-1981.*

[15]I am indebted for this formulation to Stephen Slemon's "Magic Realism as Postcolonial Discourse," quoted in Wendy Faris's "From a Far Source Within," in her book, *Ordinary Enchantments: Magical Realism and the Remystification of Narrative*, 48, note 18.

[16]William Spindler, "Magic Realism: A Typology," *Forum for Modern Language Studies*, 29:1 (1993: Jan.) 75.

[17]A revered historical figure, Tudor Vladimirescu was engaged in the political scene of the early nineteenth century and died a heroic death while trying to protect the Romanian provinces' territorial and political interests. Although originally on the side of the Greek movement known as the Eteria, whose members were seeking to overthrow the Ottoman Empire's occupation of Greece through an alliance with tsarist Russia, Tudor refused to join forces with them after realizing that both the Greeks and the Russians were using the Romanian provinces. Ţara Românească and Moldova, as a pawn that was to be sacrificed and offered to the Russian tsar after the Turks would be defeated. As a result of what was perceived as a betrayal, the leaders of the Eteria ordered Tudor's murder. In Agopian's novel, the unlikely trio composed of Boyar Lăpai, the Dwarf, and a very young Tache attempt to join Tudor's forces, unaware that he has already been murdered and his men, known as *panduri*, have already been dispersed.

[18]Romanian dictionaries define the name "Mamona" as designating both the Devil and devilish practices. The word is used, not accidentally, in Titus Popovici's novel *Setea* (The Thirst) by a character named Gavrilă al Ursului, who is a neo protestant preacher in his village.

[19]In this context, see Rosemary Jackson, *Fantasy in Literature of Subversion*, in which she argues that the goal of magical realism is to make visible the unseen and to articulate the un-said (48).

[20]For a detailed discussion of magical realism as compensatory fiction, see especially Scott Sipkins "Magical Tragedies: The Supplement of Realism" and Molly Monet-Viera "Post-Boom Magical Realism: Appropriations and Transformations of a Genre." Both authors argue

that magical realism becomes a futile mode that isolates the characters and prevents them from understanding the reality of their own country.

[21]For further elaboration on this point, see Valdez-Moses's "Magic Realism at World's End."

WORKS CITED

Agopian, Ştefan. *Velvet Tache*. Trans. Ileana Alexandra Orlich. Bucureşti: Paideia, 2008.

Anderson, Benedict. *Imagined Communities. Reflections on the Origins and Spread of Nationalism.* London: Verso and New Left Books, 1983.

Anton, Eugenia Tudor. "Postfaţa." *Drumul ascuns*. Bucureşti: Minerva, 1985.

Arghir, Sorin. Preface. *Patul lui Procust*. By Petrescu. Bucureşti: Editura de Stat pentru Literatură şi Artă, 1957.

Arzubide, Germàn List. *El movimiento estridentista*. Jalapa, Mexico: Horizonte, 1927.

Bălan, Ion Dodu. *Concise History of Romanian Literature*. Trans. Andrei Bantaş. Bucharest: Editura enciclopedică şi ştiinţifică, 1981.

Bălcescu, Nicolae. *Cuvânt preliminariu despre izvoarele istoriei românilor*. Bucureşti: Colegiul Naţional, 1845.

Barthes, Roland. *The Pleasures of the Text*. New York: Farrar, 1975.

Baudelaire, Charles. "The Painter of Modern Life." *Les Fleurs du Mal*. Trans. C. F. MacIntyre. Berkeley: University of California Press, 1947. 105.

Beaujour, Michel. "*Qu'est-ce que Nadja?*" *French Studies*, XX (1966), 366-387.

Betsk, Aaron. *Building Sex: Men, Women, Architecture, and the Construction of Sexuality*. New York: William Morrow and Company Inc., 1995.

Blaga, Lucian. *Spaţiul Mioritic, Trilogia culturii* [The Trilogy of Culture]. Bucureşti: Editura pentru Literatură Universală, 1969. 119-31.

Bordwell, David. *Narration in the Fiction Film*. Madison: University of Wisconsin Press, 1985.

Bottigheimer, Ruth B. "Silenced Women in the Grimm Tales: The

'Fit' between Fairy Tales and Society in Their Historical Context." *Fairy Tales and Society: Illusion, Allusion, and Paradigm.* Ed. Bottigheimer. Philadelphia: University of Pennsylvania Press, 1986. 115-131.

Breton, André. *Manifestoes of Surrealism.* Trans. Richard Seaver and Helen R. Lane. Ann Arbor: University of Michigan Press, 1969.

---. *Les vases communicants.* Paris: Gallimard, 1970.

---. *Nadja.* Trans. Richard Howard. New York: Grove Press, 1960.

Brook, James. "Contestarea poetică. Interviu cu Gellu Naum. "*Observatorul Cultural*, Nr. 1 (2000).

Brooker, Jewel Spears and Joseph Bentley. "Unifying Incompatible Worlds: The Sybil of Cumae and Tiresias." *Reading The Waste Land: Modernism and the Limits of Interpretation.* Amherst: University of Massachusetts Press, 1990. 14-34.

Buci-Glucksmann, Christine. *Baroque Reason: The Aesthetics of Modernity.* Trans. Patrick Camiller. London: Sage, 1994. 49.

Buelens, Gert. "Henry James Oblique Possession: Plottings of Desire and Mastery in *The American Scene.*" *PMLA* 116 2 (March 2001): 300-13.

Butler, Judith P. *Gender Trouble: Feminism and the Subversion of Identity.* New York: Routledge, 1999.

---. "Imitation and Gender Insubordination." *Inside/Out: Lesbian Theories, Gay Theories.* Ed. Diana Fuss, New York: Routledge, 1991. 13-31.

Călinescu, George. *History of Romanian Literature.* Trans. Leon Levițchi. Milan: UNESCO NAGARD Publishers, 1988.

---. *Istoria literaturii române de la origini până în prezent.* București: Fundația Regală pentru Literatură si Artă. 1941.

---. *Adevărul literar și artistic.* Seria II, an X, 22 (May 1932): 7.

Carpentier, Alejo. "On the Marvelous Real in America." Faris and Zamora. 75-88.

---. "The Baroque and the Marvelous Real." Faris and Zamora. 89 108.

Chaucer, Geoffrey. *The Canterbury Tales*. New York: Penguin Classics, 2003.

Chihaia, Pavel. *Arta medievală II. Invăţături şi mituri in Ţara Românească*. Bucureşti: Albatros, 1998. 223.

Ciopraga, Constantin. *The Personality of Romanian Literature*. Trans. Ştefan Avadănei. Iaşi: Juminea Publishing House, 1981.

Cioran, Emil. *Breviaire de vaincus*. Trans. Alain Paruit. Paris: Gallimard, 1993.

Cooper, John Xiros. *T. S. Eliot and the Politics of Voice*. Ann Arbor: UMI Research Press, 1987.

Crohmălniceanu, Ovid S. "Gellu Naum 1915-2001." *Plural: Hot Black Ink: Modernist Idiosyncrasies: Urmuz, Mateiu, Blechner, Fondane, Naum*. Bucharest: The Romanian Cultural Institute, 3, 19 (2003): 197.

Cusick, Suzanne. "Feminist Theory, Music Theory, and the Mind/Body Problem." *Perspectives of New Music* Vol. 32, No. 1 (Winter, 1994): 8-27.

De Gourmont, Remy. *The Natural Philosophy of Love*. Trans. Ezra Pound. New York: Rarity Press, 1931.

Doolittle, Hilda (H.D.). *Notes on Thought and Vision*. Trans. Paul Bowles. San Francisco: City Lights, 2001.

Dreiser, Theodore. *Sister Carrie*. New York: Doubleday, 1900.

Eisner, Lotte H. *The Haunted Screen: Expressionism in the German Cinema and the Influence of Max Reinhardt*. Trans. Roger Greaves, London: Thames and Hudson, 1969.

Eliade, Mircea. *The Fate of Romanian Culture*. Trans. Bogdan Ştefănescu. Bucharest: Editura Athena, 1995.

---. *Zamolxis, the Vanishing God*. Trans. Willard Trask. Chicago: University of Chicago UP, 1972.

Eliot, T. S. *The Complete Poems and Plays 1909-1950*. New York: Harcourt, Brace and Company, 1958.

---. "The Metaphysical Poets." *Selected Prose of T. S. Eliot*. Ed. Frank Kermode. New York: Harcourt Trade, 1975. 59-67.

---. "Milton II." Kermode 266.

---. "Hamlet and His Problems." *The Sacred Wood and Major Early Essays*. New York: Dover Publications, Inc., 1997. 58.

---. "Tradition and the Individual Talent." *The Sacred Wood*. 31.

---. *Selected Essays of T. S. Eliot*. New York: Harcourt, Brace and World, Inc., 1964.

---. "Lecture I: Toward a Definition of a Metaphysical Poetry." *The Varieties of Metaphysical Poetry*. Ed. Ronald Schuschard. New York: Harcourt Brace and Company, 1993.

---. *The Waste Land: A Facsimile and Transcript of the Original Drafts*. Ed. Valerie Eliot. London: Faber and Faber, 1971.

---. *The Waste Land and Other Poems*. New York: Harcourt, Brace and Company, 1962.

Ellis, Havelock. *Studies in the Psychology of Sex*. Vol. I. Philadelphia: F. A. Davis Company, Publishers, 1913.

Emerson, Ralph Waldo. *Essays and Lectures*. New York: Library of America, 1983.

Faris, Wendy. *Ordinary Echantments: Magical Realism and the Remystification of Narrative*. Nashville: Vanderbilt University Press, 2004.

---. "Scheherazade's Children: Magical Realism and Postmodern Fiction." Faris and Zamora. 163-190.

Felman, Schoshana. "Review: Women and Madness: The Critical\ Phallacy." *Diacritics* Vol. 5, No. 4 (Winter 1975): 2-10.

Flores, Angel. "Magical Realism in Spanish American Fiction." *Hispania* 38, 2 (May 1955): 187-192.

Fondane, Benjamin. *Privelişti*. Piteşti: Editura Paralela, 2002.

Foucalt, Michel. "The Father's 'No'". *Aesthetics, Method and Epistemology*. Ed. J. Faubion. Trans. Donald F. Bouchard and Sherry Simon. New York: New Press, 1989.

---. "Revolutionary Action: Until Now." *Language, Counter Memory, Practice*. Ithaca: Cornell University Press, 1980. 218-33.

Frazer, James. *The Golden Bough: A Study in Magic and Religion*. New York: Oxford University Press, 1998.

Freud, Sigmund. "The Interpretation of Dreams." *The Standard Edition of the Complete Psychological Works*. Vol. 4, Ed. James Strachey. New York: W. W. Norton & Company, 2000. 149.

Fridan, Betty. *The Feminine Mystique*. New York: Dell Books, 1963.

Frye, Northrop. *The Secular Scripture*. Cambridge, MA: Harvard University Press, 1976.

Gaines, James R. *Evening in the Palace of Reason*. New York: Harper Collins, 2005.

Gauthier, Xavière. *Surréalisme et sexualité*. Paris: Gallimard, 1971.

Gauthier, Xavière. *Poésies complètes*. Paris: Bibliothèque-Charpentier, 1905.

Georgescu, Paul. "Frumuseţea adevărului." *Printre cărţi*. Bucureşti: Editura Eminescu, 1973.

---. "Clasicismul creator." *Printre cărţi*. Bucureşti: Editura Eminescu, 1973.

Georgescu, Vlad. *The Romanians: A History*. Ed. Matei Călinescu. Trans. Alexandra Bley-Vroman. Columbus: Ohio State Press, 1991. 205.

Gilbert, Sandra M. and Susan Gubar. *No Man's Land: The Place of the Woman Writer in the Twentieth Century*. Vol. 2. New Haven: Yale University Press, 1989.

Halttunen, Karen. *Confidence Men and Painted Women: A Study of Middle-Class Culture in America, 1830-1870*. New Haven: Yale UP, 1982.

Hebbel, Friedrich. Introduction. *Maria Magdalena*. By Hebbel. *Masterpieces of the Modern German Theatre*. Trans. Carl Richard Mueller. Ed. Robert W. Corrigan. New York: Collier, 1967.

Holban, Anton. *Azi*, an I, no. 3-4 (1932).

Hulme, Peter. Introduction. *Discourse/Postcolonial Theory*. Ed. Hulme, Francis Barker, and Margaret Iversen. Manchester: Manchester University Press, 1994. 14.

Iorga, Nicolae. *Istoria Literaturii Romane in secolul al XVIII-lea* 1901 2 Vols. Bucharest: Minerva, 1901.

Iragaray, Luce. "La Mystérique." *Speculum of Another Woman*. Trans. Gillian C. Gill. Ithaca: Cornell University Press, 1984.

---. *The Irigaray Reader*. Ed. Margaret Whitford. Oxford: Blackwell, 1991.

---. *Ce sexe qui n'en est pas us*. Paris: Minuit, 1977.

J. D. "Notes on Thought and Vision." *The Gender of Modernism*. Ed. Bonnie Kime Scott. Bloomington: Indiana University Press, 1990. 108.

Jackson, Rosemary. *Fantasy in Literature of Subversion*. New York: Routledge, 1981.

James, Henry. *Henry James Letters, Vol. 4: 1895-1916*. Cambridge: Belknap Press, 1984.

Judovitz, Dalia. *The Culture of the Body: Genealogies of Modernity*. Ann Arbor: The University of Michigan Pres, 2004.

Kayser, Wolfgang. *Das Groteske in Malerei und Dichtung*. Hamburg: Rowohlt, 1960.

Kenyon, Linda. "A Conversation with Robert Kroetsch." *New Quarterly* 5 (Spring 1985): 15.

Korg, Jacob. "Modern Art Techniques." Martin 87.

Kristeva, Julia. *Revolution in Poetic Language*. Trans. Margaret Waller. New York: Columbia University Press, 1984.

---. *Powers of Horror: An Essay in Abjection.* Trans. Leon S. Roudiez. New York: Columbia University Press, 1983.

Ladimer, Bethany. "Madness and the Irrational in the Works of André Breton: A Feminist Perspective." *Feminist Studies*, Vol. 6, No. 1 (Spring 1980): 175-95.

Lamm, Martin. *Modern Drama.* Trans. Karen Elliott. New York: Philosophical Library, 1953.

Latham, Ernest H. *Mioriţa: An Icon of Romanian Culture.* Iaşi: The Center for Romanian Studies, 1999.

Leal, Luis. "Magical Realism in Spanish American Literature." Faris and Zamora. 119-124.

Lopez, Alfred J. *Posts and Pasts: A Theory of Postcolonialism.* Albany: SUNY Press, 2001.

Lovinescu, Eugen. *Istoria literaturii române* 6 vols. Bucureşti:

---. *Istoria literaturii române contemporane, 1900-1937.* Bucureşti: Socec, 1937.

Lovinescu, Monica. "*Est-etice/Unde scurte IV.*" Bucureşti: Humanitas, 1994.

Lynes, Carlos. "Surrealism and the Novel." *French Studies* XX (1966): 366-387.

Mann, Thomas. *The Magic Mountain.* Trans. H. T. Lowe-Porter. London: Secker and Wargurg, 1927.

Manolescu, Nicolae. *Istoria critică a literaturii române.* Bucureşti: Minerva, 1990.

Marcuse, Herbert. *Eros and Civilization.* Boston: Beacon Press, 1974.

Martin, Jay, ed. *A Collection of Critical Essays on "The Waste Land".* Englewood Cliffs: Prentice Hall, 1968.

McMullin, Stanley "'Adam's Mad in Eden': Magic Realism as Hinterland Experience." *Magic Realism and Canadian Literature: Essays and Stories. Proceedings of the Conference on Magic Realist Writing in Canada.* Eds. Peter Hinchcliffe and Ed Jewinski. Waterloo, ON: University of Waterloo Press, 1986, 13-22.

Menton, Seymor. *Magic Realism Rediscovered 1918-1981*. Philadelphia: Art Alliance Press, 1983.

Merleau-Ponty, Maurice. *The Phenomenology of Perception*. Trans. Colin Smith. London: Routledge and Kegan Paul, 1995. 408.

---. "Flesh of the World – Flesh of the Body – Being." *The Visible and the Invisible*. By Merleau-Ponty. Trans. Alphonso Lingis. Evanston: Northwest University Press, 1968. 248-50.

Micu, Dimitru. *Istoria literaturii române: De la creația populară la post Modernism*. București: Saeculum I. O, 2000.

Moi, Toril. *Sexual Textual Politics*. London: Routledge, 1985, 140.

Monet-Viera, Molly. "Post-Boom Magical Realism: Appropriations and Transformations of a Genre." *Revista de Estudios Hispanicos*. Vol. 38 1 (2004) 95-117.

Monléon, José. *A Specter is Haunting Europe: A Sociohistorical Approach to the Fantastic*. Princeton, NJ: Princeton University Press, 1990.

Moses, Michael Valdez. "Magic Realism at World's End." *Literary Imagination: The Review of the Association of Literary Scholars and Critics* 3 (2001): 105-33.

Motherwell, Robert. *The Dada Painters and Poets: An Anthology*. New York: Wittenborn, Schultz, 1951.

Muthu, Mircea. "'Haiducul' in literaturile sud-europene." *Revista de istorie și teorie literară* 32.3 (July-September 1984): 68-73.

Naum, Gellu. *Zenobia (Writings from an Unbound Europe)*. Trans. James Brook and Sasha Vlad. Evanston: Northwest University Press, 1995.

Negrici, Eugen. Prefața. *Tache de catifea* Buchurești: Polirom, 2004. 5-11.

Nicholls, Peter. *Modernism: A Literary Guide*. Berkeley: University of California Press, 1995.

Nietsche, Friedrich. "The Twilight of Idols." *The Twilight of the Idols and The Anti-Christ: or How to Philosophize with a Hammer*. Ed. Michael Tanner. Trans. R. J. Hollingate. New York: Penguin Classics, 1990.

---. *Untimely Meditations*. Trans. R. J. Hollingdale. Ed. Hollingdale. Cambridge: Cambridge University Press, 1997.

Ong, Walter J. *Orality and Literacy: The Technologizing of the World*. New York: Routledge, 1982.

Orlich, Ileana Alexandra. *Silent Bodies: (Re)Discovering the Women of Romanian Short Fiction*. New York: Columbia University Press, 2002.

Papadat-Bengescu, Hortensia. *The Disheveled Maidens*. Trans. Ileana Alexandra Orlich. Bucharest: The Romanian Cultural Institute Publishing House, 2004.

---. *A Concert of Music by Bach*. Trans. Ileana Alexandra Orlich. Craiova: Scrisul românesc, Fundaţia Editura, 2005.

---. *The Hidden Way*. Trans. Ileana Alexandra Orlich. Craiova: Scrisul românesc, Fundaţia Editura, 2007.

Papahagi, Marian. "In căutarea sensului ascuns." *Cumpănă şi semn*. Bucureşti: Cartea românească, 1990. 36-42.

Peiss, K. "Making Up and Making Over: Cosmetics, Consumer Culture, and Women's Identity." *The Sex of Things: Gender and Consumption in Historical Perspective*. Ed. V. de Grazia. Berkeley, CA: University of California Press, 1996. 311-36.

Petrescu, Camil. *Patul lui Procust*. Bucureşti: Editura de Stat pentru Literatură şi Artă, 1957.

---. *The Bed of Procrustes*. Trans. Ileana Alexandra Orlich. Bucharest: Editura Fundaţia Camil Petrescu, 2008.

Poirier, Richard. "Panoramic Environment and the Anonymity of the Self." *Sister Carrie*. By Theodore Dreiser. Norton Critical Edition. Ed. Donald Pizer. New York: Norton, 1970: 583.

Pop, Ion. *Gellu Naum – poezia contra literaturii*. Cluj: Casa Cărţii de Ştiinţă, 2001.

Popescu, Simona. "Salvarea speciei. Despre suprarealism şi Gellu

Naum. Bucureşti: Editura Fundaţiei Culturale, 2000.

Pound, Ezra. "In a Station of the Metro." Modern American Poetry. Ed. Louis Utermeyer. New York: Harcourt, Brace and company, 1921.

Rapaneau, Valeriu. "Armonii statice şi necesare." *Drumul ascuns: Prefaţă, Curriculum vitae şi Bibliografie*. Bucureşti: Editura 100+1 Gramar, 1990.

Rich, Adrienne. "Notes toward a Politics of Location." *Blood, Bread and Poetry: Selected Prose 1979 -1985*. New York: W. W. Norton & Company, 1986.

Richards, I. A. "Critiques." Martin 44.

Roh, Franz. "Magic Realism: Post-Expressionists." *Magical Realism*. Eds. L. P. Zamora and W. B. Faris. Durham: Duke UP, 1995. 15-32.

Sadoveanu, Mihail. *The Hatchet*. Trans. Eugenia Farca. *Classics of Romanian Literature*, Volume III. New York: East European Monographs, 1991.

---. *Tales from Ancuţa's Inn*. Trans. Ileana Alexandra Orlich. Bucharest: The Romanian Cultural Institute Publishing House, 2004.

Scott, Joan Wallach. "Gender: A Useful Category of Historical Analysis." *Gender and the Politics of History*. New York: Columbia University Press, 1988, 28-50.

Sedgwick, Eve Kosofsky. *Between Men: English Literature and Male Homosocial Desire*. New York: Columbia University Press, 1985.

Shaw, George Bernard. *Heartbreak House*. Harmondsworth: Penguin, 1964.

Showalter, Elaine. *Sexual Anarchy, Gender and Culture at the Fin de Siècle*. London: Virago, 1995.

Sipkins, Scott. "Magical Strategies: The Supplement of Realism." *Twentieth Century Literature* 34.2 (Summer 1988): 140-154.

Slemon, Stephen. "Magic Realism as Postcolonial Discourse."

Canadian Literature 116 (Spring 1988): 9-24.

Sontag, Susan. *Illness as Metaphor*. New York: Farrar, Straus and Giroux, 1978. 43.

Spivak, Gayatri Chakravorty. "Can the Subaltern Speak?" *Marxism and the Interpretation of Culture*. Eds. Cary Nelson and Lawrence Grossberg. Urbana: University of Illinois Press, 1988.

Spindler, William. "Magic Realism: A Typology." *Forum for Modern Language Studies* 29:1 (Jan. 1993): 75.

Stoppard, Tom. *Travesties*. New York: Grove Press, 1975.

Street, Brian V. *Literacy in Theory and Practice*. Cambridge: Cambridge UP, 1984, 110.

Symonds, John Addington. *Renaissance in Italy*. New York: H. Holt, 1888. 274.

Tate, Allen. "The Fire Sermon." Martin 32-3.

Templeton, Joan. "Fallen Women and Upright Wives: "Women's Place in Early Modern Tragedy." *Reconfigured Spheres: Feminist Explorations of Literary Spaces*. Eds. Margaret R. Higonnet and Joan Templeton. Amherst: University of Massachusetts Press, 1994. 60-71.

Tzara, Tristan. *Lampisteries précedées des sept manifestes dada*. Paris: Jean-Jacques Pauvert, 1963.

---. "*Le pouvoir des images*." *Oeuvres Complètes* Tome 4 1947-1963. Paris: Fammarion, 1980.

Waldeck, R. G. *Athéné Palace*. New York: Robert M. McBride & Co., 1942.

Weston, Jessie. *From Ritual to Romance*. Cambridge U. Press, 1920.

Woolf, Virginia. "On Being Ill." *The Essays of Virginia Woolf, Volume IV (1925-1928)*.
London: Hogarth Press, 1986. 317-8.

Young, David, and Keith Hollaman. *Magical Realist Fiction: An Anthology*. Oberlin: Oberlin College Press, 1984.

Zăvăleanu, Laura. "A Descent into the Field of Histories: Between the Strictures of Science and the Generosity of Myth." *Transylvanian Review* Vol. XV 3 (Fall 2006).